D1130317

HUMANISTIC PSYCHIATRY:
FROM OPPRESSION TO CHOICE

HUMANISTIC PSYCHIATRY: FROM OPPRESSION TO CHOICE

ROY D. WALDMAN, M.D.

RUTGERS UNIVERSITY PRESS

NEW BRUNSWICK, NEW JERSEY

Copyright © 1971 by Rutgers University, the State University
of New Jersey

Library of Congress Catalog Card Number: 78–138424

SBN: 8135–0681–6

Manufactured in the United States of America

Portions of this book have appeared in *The American Journal of Psycho-therapy*, *The Psychoanalytic Review*, *The American Journal of Orthopsy-chiatry*, and *The Journal of Individual Psychology*

The author is grateful to the publishers for permission to quote from the following:

"Equality of Opportunity as a Cultural Value" from "Aspects of Human Equality," Fifteenth Symposium of the Conference on Science, Philosophy and Religion, in *Freedom and Culture*, by Dorothy Lee, published by Prentice Hall, Inc., 1956; *The Social Psychology of George Herbert Mead*, by G. H. Mead, University of Chicago Press, 1964; *Patterns of Culture*, by Ruth Benedict, Houghton Mifflin Company, 1934; *Black Skin, White Masks*, by Frantz Fanon, Grove Press, Inc., 1967; *The Penal Colony*, by Franz Kafka, Schocken Books, 1948; *The Traitor*, by André Gorz (Foreword by J. J. Sartre), John Calder, Ltd.; *The Desert*, by Allen B. Wheelis, Basic Books, Inc., 1960.

To Karmela

CONTENTS

PREFACE

Idioms of "health," "sickness," and "treatment" are often the means by which the psychiatric problem is successfully isolated and screened from the challenges of life by both physician and patient. I therefore propose in this work to consider so-called mental illness as *central* rather than *incidental* to the three dimensions—individual, social, and existential—of life. The patient, in keeping with the manner in which he perceives the demands of his life situation, and who has already committed himself to avenues of refuge and escape and logically finds these idioms convenient, is perhaps unaware that he unwittingly compounds his problem in perpetually neglecting the demands of existence. The mental health worker, for his part limited by his naturalistic–medical framework, is inclined to further compound this dilemma. As an instance, has not psychoanalysis replaced one reductionistic viewpoint with another of its own? Has it not substituted for the unambiguous phobia which the patient believes responsible for his dilemma an alternative explanation reducible to a matter of sexual and aggressive instincts? It is with such explanations that both patient and therapist too often close themselves off from the radical realities of existence; indeed, a most curious occurrence in consideration of the psychoanalytic exhortation in so far as is concerned the ominous effect of both repression and illusion.

It will be my task in this work to introduce a *humanistic* alternative to the *mechanistic* one that continues to permeate the field of mental health. It is an alternative that may allow for the unfolding of both psychiatric theory and practice in terms of the problems of life itself rather than the reverse. The task before us becomes one of translating the psychiatric problem from an impersonal–naturalistic framework to a humanistic, personal one. It is a two-fold one. The symptom or problem of the patient first must be regarded as subjective, creative, and purposeful, albeit beyond his awareness. Responsibility and intent of the patient—at the risk of seeming harsh —must not be minimized. We shall otherwise beset ourselves with a myriad of inconsistencies and logical impasses that would impede the development of our theoretical propositions throughout this work. More important, we shall be obscuring precisely that which we are desirous of clarifying—the realities and possibilities of man's freedom. And second, if we are to agree that the symptom is purposeful we must then investigate the conditions of existence that prompt man so to pervert his freedom. For in fact what we commonly refer to as mental illness is simply one manifestation of man's lost freedom. Why is man beset with the plight and misery as expressed by his particular psychiatric problem? Is it *accidental* or *imposed?* The answer can be found by nothing short of a thorough inquiry into the three dimensions of human existence.

I therefore intend this work to serve for the beginning student or layman interested in problems of man and "mental health" as an orientation to the means by which the psychiatric problem may be understood in terms of the life of man writ large. To the advanced student it may serve as an incentive to plot in further detail the coordinates that link man, his world, and God in the interests of allowing man to enact the ennobling possibilities of which he is capable. That we have thus far failed in this task is signaled in one aspect by the prevalence of mental illness, which in itself further testifies to man's losing struggle with his *sociohistorical predicament* and not to *any accidents of biology.*

Roy D. Waldman, M.D.

New Brunswick, New Jersey
June 1970

HUMANISTIC PSYCHIATRY:

FROM OPPRESSION TO CHOICE

HUMAN NATURE

 *Chapter 1*

THE PROBLEM OF EXISTENCE

Man's existence is limited in that he cannot be other than free; he can choose all except not to choose.

> "Human reality can choose itself as it intends but it is not able not to choose itself." [1]

Man's reality is his choice. His existence is not to be taken for granted. He is obliged to choose his reality at every moment and is therefore not once and for all sad, depressed, or anxious in the way "a table is a table."

Human existence is neither made nor determined by the laws of physical nature. If it were so man would not be free. As man is forced to choose and exercise his freedom, conscience, doubt, and perplexity never cease to plague him. His existence is therefore a continual puzzle and riddle to himself. Man's destiny and condition make it unavoidable that in all his actions his choice between evil and good is inevitable.

Human action taken to avoid, postpone, or evade the effort and risk of maximizing one's freedom has commonly led man to the brink of misery and self-destruction. The common pre-

3

occupation with violence and power on both the collective and individual planes appears to be a preferable diversion from the challenge of destiny—the risk of freedom. Man's concern for power and violence offers a convenient distraction from the responsibilities of freedom; its ramifications and significance will be a focal point of this work. An example of such distraction is what we refer to as mental illness—one possible outcome of man's perennial flight from the responsibilities of freedom.

IN AND BEYOND NATURE

The task of man—his existence—must be considered as simply a *possibility* rather than his *destiny* as in the case of the animal which is confined wholly within the grasp of nature. As part of man's task it is necessary for him to create, innovate, and originate and thus transcend the blind automatic laws of nature's cycle. Man, whose actions transcend the physical laws of nature, cannot be significantly understood if we are to apply to him the very objectifying techniques of the physical sciences that have served well to comprehend and control nature.

In contrast to animals enmeshed within the ahistorical cycles of nature—who have always been what they are today—man *has* and *is* his history. It is only in the realization of the significance and impact of history that we are able to take cognizance of man's possibility to create. A historical actor need not be what he has been nor must he be tomorrow what he is today. The history of man may be viewed as the steps he has taken from and toward the path of truth, justice, and responsibility. That obviously is of no concern in the study of animal behavior.

For creatures of nature who already are what they are and will forever remain so, it is meaningless to speak of truth and justice. Only man is free to choose and decide; it is therefore only for man that the concept of truth, justice, and responsibility have relevance. As man is uncertain[2] of his actions, he must continually seek to sustain himself by reliance on criteria of truth and justice. A search for truth therefore only has meaning to man the animal who is not yet established and who comes into being with the truth he uncovers. As ultimate truth is a divine prerogative, man's task is always unfinished. His world is as incomplete as the animal's world is complete and for whom there is no need to be concerned with truth and justice.

It is from such perspectives that we may strive to differentiate man from animal. It is also by way of these perspective that I intend to focus upon the problems of man and mental illness in an effort to interpret them in the light of the problem of *human existence* rather than as *happenings of nature*.

VIOLATION OF FREEDOM

Man is all too often unaware that life is given to him empty; it is for free man to fill for himself. Every moment has its possibilities. As has been said, each man is Adam anew. Each generation is unique. Each must decide from the beginning. As there is not a fixed human nature, man's nature is his choice. It is not determined as is the sound of music of the phonograph.

As man is free

. . . nothingness, is coiled in his being as a snail in its shell.[3]

The existence of Nothing between man's motives and his actions—between his past and his present; between his feelings and his conduct—attests to man's freedom. Condemned to this condition he is by necessity insecure—his thoughts uncertain, his actions marked by doubt. He has on the one hand the possibility to be himself. On the other he may say no to his existence.

Nevertheless, the condition of freedom and choice is inevitably the condition of man. In contrast to the animal who is forever what he is, man can choose to forfeit his manhood. He is able to violate his freedom as a condition of this very freedom. Man is able to violate his freedom in a variety of ways. Two such ways, sin and neuroses as well as their interrelationship, will be depicted later in this work. The apparent intricacies and bizarreness of what is referred to as mental illness may easily be interpreted within the framework of man's condition of freedom. There is, in other words, no *cause* per se to be "discovered" for the phenomena of mental illness. Is mental illness simply one of man's many choices by which he eschews the task of freedom, truth, and responsibility? Yes! Nevertheles, it is a choice only fully comprehensible in view of the totality of his circumstance and social context: his total life situation.

The loss of man's humanity—his abdication from freedom— is signaled by the dichotomy between his action and his thoughts. The essence of humanity on the other hand lies in the synthesis of the highest form of action and thought—love and intelligence—without which neither freedom nor responsibility may be sustained. It is the condition of man's freedom—his situation—in face of the risks and perplexities of life that tempts him to ostensibly simplify his life task in avoiding this synthesis and thereby separate thought from action. Thought and action separated from each other become ends in themselves. It is when thought becomes an end in itself that we confront man in his powerless condition of neurosis and psychosis.[4] It is when action becomes an end in itself that we confront man in the mirror-image condition of sin where he has aggrandized his power. As we shall see (chapter 8), he is free in neither situation.

The separation of thought from action may be depicted as a basic evasion of human responsibility. Thought without action and conversely action without thought is the means by which man believes he can overcome the risk of awareness, decision, and choice. By means of such separation he erroneously believes himself able to minimize the risks of responsibility required of him by the demands of existence. He seeks to transfer or evade such responsibility in both his individual and collective actions (chapter 6).

The inherent realities of life, of which man is often unaware, are such that his existence is absolutely untransferable.[5] This simple but important concept—the notion that life is untransferable ought to be understood from at least three basic perspectives. First, man is inevitably encased in or "nailed to his body." It is this condition of enforced solitude that makes him inescapably responsible for his bodily actions. Second, man as a "being" must unavoidably maintain interest in his "being"; the uniqueness as well as the importance of his "being" is stamped into his bones and is therefore untransferable. Third, death—perhaps more than anything else—suggests that man's existence is untransferable. Both Life and Death must be confronted. It is only the terms and meaning of one's life and death that are at issue.

THE OTHER IN SITUATION

We have thus far pointed to the burden of freedom rather abstractly—devoid of the Other; devoid of situation. If, however, we are to come to an understanding of man—if we will be able to decipher the enigma of his existence—we cannot continue to confront him as an isolated self. He must, as the existentialist would have it, be considered as a "being in the world." It is only in the dialogue between men that man is able to exercise his true freedom. Conversely, the absence or avoidance of dialogue is part of man's attempt to evade responsibility for his existence. As we shall see, it is by means of tactics of power or powerlessness, wherein he falsely believes that he is able to obviate such dialogue together with the anguish of choices and decisions and thereby eliminate the risks of freedom.

Whether I am free or not depends upon my actions within a situation. I become who I am only if I resist the oppressiveness of the Other. It is only in a situation that I must confront the Other and in which the peril, anguish, and responsibility of choice and freedom becomes a matter for concern. Ortega's comments depict the reasons for the precariousness of my predicament in a situation with the Other:

> You have a mode of being that is your own and peculiar to you and does not coincide with mine. From you arise frequent negations of my being—of my way of thinking of feeling of wanting and desiring.[6]

We are hence forcefully carried to the realization that our life situation is inseparable from the threat of oppression and uncertainty.

It is both contingency and oppressive reality, which man is fearful of confronting, that often prompt him to prepare the groundwork for his retreat. It is the tragedy of man that he learns too late, if ever, that retreat and abdication from freedom are not fruitful prerogatives. As existence is untransferable, risk becomes unavoidable. The meaning of man's life may be viewed in the context of whether he openly seeks to confront or furtively seeks to avoid this challenge. It is a central theme of this work to point to the dire consequences of such avoidance.

It is thus the appearance of the Other that awakens man's responsibility to the precariousness of his existence. The arrival of the Other further provides him with the temptation to utilize this Other in an effort to provide himself with the illusion of hiding from the demands of existence: confrontation, risk, and responsibility. It is the anguish and risk of freedom and choice in face of the Other, therefore, that tempt man to employ diversionary tactics of power and violence that I believe characterize the relations between man and man as well as that of between nations.

MAN AND FICTION

Man may act only within a situation. His particular mode of action, as well as the situation in which he finds himself, reflects the arbitrary fictional nature of his world. The concept of man as a fictional animal wherein all human action is merely a possibility provides the esence of the meaning of freedom for the human creature.

The world of each man is simply one reality carved out of endless possibilities.[7] For example,

> In the Western world, we have in our system of thought, notions and attitudes which predispose us to evaluation in terms of equality. Assessment and even apprehension of objects of knowledge in terms of comparison, is fundamental to our thinking. We know that a thing is good because we recognize it as good as or better than; we know that an infant is tall or slow only when we know his age, that is, when we can compare him with the infants in his age-group. We define according to similarities and dissimilarities, according to qualities which can be analyzed and abstracted out of the field under consideration. For example, John Plamenatz writes: "Everyone knows that, whatever the respect in which we choose to compare men, some will be superior to others." This may be true when we do choose certain respects in which to compare men. But *there are societies where*

no one is "superior to others," not because the goal of equality has been successfully achieved, not because all men are born with equal ability, but because two fundamental premises necessary to this proposition are lacking: the notion of comparison is not present, and neither is the practice of choosing a "respect" out of the totality of the individual. [P. 42]

People desire to be good (or rather good-gardeners); not better than. A gardener works much and hard because he was strong, because he enjoyed gardening, because he wanted to participate largely in the gift-giving situations. Neither he nor others made a practice of evaluating his work against a comparative standard of achievement for expectation. *Striving was not for equality nor for superiority; it was for the enhancement of uniqueness* [italics mine]. [P. 43]

Nevertheless, for most men the world in which they live is as real as the solid earth upon which they tread rather than an invented artifact of one's culture. The world of man is taken for granted by one who is born into a particular situation comprised of institutions and values which unavoidably influence his orientation in both time and space. He is, as well, provided with a past and future into which this present world is snugly and realistically fitted.

In spite of the harshness and apparent realness of man's world it must be recalled that for the most part it is an arbitrary one. I mean by fictional and arbitrary—specifically—that man's way of life in the world—his customs, language and every day ways—are not at all reducible to physical dimensions. The physical deterministic parameters of neither his physiology, nor his geography, nor his climate will tell us what is essential about man, history, and society.

If we may speak loosely of the "destiny" of man the fictional animal, it is that he alone must chart the course and ways from which his life will take direction. His destiny is that he is unable to rely upon his instinctual endowment to accomplish this task. Bereft of an adequate instinctual make-up, man thus is denied the certainty of a ready-made world. His world then must be carved out of the arbitrary designs of human creativity.

Human ways may be considered to be fictional in that as they are not reducible to physical dimensions; they are unavoidably arbitrary as in Pascal's aphorism that "what constitutes truth on one side of the Pyrenees is error on the other side." We are now able to arrive at the conclusion that human concepts, thoughts, ideas, and actions are not at all intended to mirror or reproduce physical reality. Neither are they simply arbitrary but more concisely they are purposeful in that they enable man to act in the world of his choice.[8] In this sense human action is not at all akin to physical happenings that can be explained in reference to the natural world of causality. The conduct of man must be interpreted and comprehended on the basis of its meaning within the context of a particular cultural framework. All feelings, thoughts, and actions are therefore the very creation of man and depend on purpose and meaning within the context of the sociohistorical setting. In fact, as I shall have occasion to note below, it is the very task of psychotherapy to concern itself with and thereby unravel the hidden meaning of man's actions.

The view of man as a fictional animal allows us to conceptualize human action as one alternative amongst others. It allows for the development of a perspective that enables one to distinguish between the natural world and the human world. The former world just "is"; the latter is a value-laden historical one. Established institutionalized traditions such as marriage in the West may therefore not be explained on the basis of physical necessity or instinct. But rather monogamy must be viewed as one possibility amongst others. We are obliged to distinguish in the case of man between what *is* and what *ought to be*.

ETHICAL CONCERNS

At this point we must digress to consider at least briefly the ethical and moral issues that come to the fore as an upshot of our commitment to the fictional-purposeful nature of human action. Having minimized the determinism of physical causality, if we were to consider all human actions to be arbitrary and therefore equally valid, we would be drawn into the abyss of moral relativism with all its barbaric and odious ramifications. If we are then to be able to proceed with an account of man as a fictional animal, we must at the same time not wholly ignore the moral and ethical issues that are inseparable from a study of human actions. By what criteria and standards shall we consider such actions? Criteria are necessary in that despite the fictionality of man's actions, not all conduct is equally fruitful or ennobling to the human species.

The emphasis of the physical sciences in explaining natural phenomena lies, as has been said, in the uncovering of what "is" through resorting to discovery based on the utilization of physical techniques. The moral and ethical dilemmas in the physical sciences have to do only with the conduct of the scientist or investigator—how are his discoveries in chemistry, biology, or physics to be utilized?—whereas in the social sciences there are moral consequences in so far as both "investigator" and "investigated" (people) are concerned. Ethical issues thus come more quickly to the fore. In either case, ethical judgments of human action must be based at least in one of its parameters on the outcome or consequences of such conduct. As we assume human action to be free and arbitrary, it is necessary to distinguish between what "is" and "ought to be." Only by means of such a perspective are we able to pose ethical judgment that will unavoidably confront man with the consequences of his actions. The possibility of appraising human action in terms of its significance, meaning, and consequence is inevitably linked to the conceptualization of man as a fictional animal, one who has a choice.

MAN AS A SYMBOL USER

It is within man's disposition to utilize symbols that constitute an important dimension of his fictional existence without which he would be unable to free himself from the iron laws of nature. To suggest that man is a symbolic animal means very simply that he does not live by bread alone. He immerses himself in a world of symbols that bear no relevance to any of his physiological necessities. Man by means of his indulgence in a

symbolic, artificial world commits himself to a fictional existence that is essentially divorced from the world.

To the extent that man is involved with symbols, he frees
himself from the immediate presence of nature. Symbols allow
for the transcending of the natural world; man transcends his
creaturely existence to become one who creates. He thus establishes himself as one who is in nature—one who is nailed to his
body—but at the same time is able to step beyond nature's
confinements.

It must be clear that man does not divest himself completely
of his physiological make-up; it is merely transcended as he
becomes immersed in a symbolic world of his own creation. In
other terms, man's body becomes the means by which symbolic
action is carried forward. A symbolic world is thereby grafted
upon the world of nature. Physical reality is *necessary* but,
as we can see, not at all *sufficient* to explain human action.

It is only when man's brain is not intact do we witness behavior that is nonsymbolic—a pure happening. Otherwise all
man's transactions are unavoidably enmeshed in a framework
of symbolic significance. All supposedly physiological happenings such as birth, puberty, and death, for example, are imbued
with symbolic meaning in accordance with the dictates of the
cultural setting.[9]

. . . a survey of puberty institutions makes clear a further fact:
puberty is physiologically a different matter in the life-cycle of
the male and female. If cultural emphasis followed the physiological emphasis, girls' ceremonies would be more marked than
boys'; but it is not so. The ceremonies emphasize a social fact:
the adult prerogatives of men are more far-reaching in every
culture than women's, and consequently, as in the above instances, it is more common for societies to take note of this period in boys than in girls. [P. 26]

Among the Carrier Indians of British Columbia, the fear and
horror of a girl's puberty was at its height. Her three or four
years of seclusion was called "the burying alive," and she lived
for all that time alone in the wilderness, in a hut of branches far
from all beaten trails. She was a threat to any person who might
so much as catch a glimpse of her, and her mere footstep defiled

a path or a river. She was covered with a great headdress of tanned skin that shrouded her face and breasts and fell to the ground behind. Her arms and legs were loaded with sinew bands to protect her from the evil spirit with which she was filled. She was herself in danger and she was a source of danger to everybody else. [P. 28]

While in some tribes the first menses of girls are a potent supernatural blessing, among the Apaches I have seen the priests themselves pass on their knees before the row of solemn little girls to receive from them the blessing of their touch. All the babies and the old people come also of necessity to have illness removed from them. The adolescent girls are not segregated as sources of danger, but court is paid to them as to direct sources of supernatural blessing. [P. 28–29]

The adolescent behavior, therefore, even of girls was not directed by some physiological characteristic of the period itself, but rather by marital or magic requirements socially connected with it. These beliefs made adolescence in one tribe serenely religious and beneficient, and in another so dangerously unclean that the child had to cry out in warning that others might avoid her in the woods. [P. 29]

The cycles of nature thus become heavy with human meaning. The most elementary of man's physiological necessities—eating, drinking, sleeping, and so forth—become enmeshed in a symbolic pattern of meaning. One's presence at a banquet—the drinking of wine, the company of a beautiful woman—provides man with far more than the satisfaction of elemental necessities.

Man's instinctual make-up, provided by nature, is incidental or accidental to his actions and thereby expresses his fictional-symbolic disposition. Nevertheless, man, as other creatures, is attracted by regularity, order, and security that nature provides for all its creatures. He, however, must seek to establish a measure of order and security through the designs and creativeness of his symbolic world. As such he is able to recoup part of his loss in having given up the order of the cyclical regularity of nature. It is, for example, the creation of the family unit—a principal underpinning of man's symbolic world—that expresses in multifold ways man's quest for order and regularity.

It is within the family that the child is admonished to respect the social order. The family unit itself bestows order and regularity in regard to duties and obligations. Symbolic family rituals establish order for human conduct, as in the sphere of sexuality, that nature otherwise provides within the domain of animal existence. It is by means of symbolic roles delegated to members of the family, mother, father, grandparents, and so forth, and which vary from culture to culture, that order and meaning are established in everyday tasks and duties. Variations in different cultures in regard to human sexual conduct, for instance, come about by arbitrary design and invention rather than through passive evolutionary natural processes.

Man may therefore be conceptualized as one who has a body by means of which he enacts symbolic designs rather than as an animal who simply is a body. It is the latter that reacts not to symbols but to signals that are a part of his natural world. Such signals may be changes in season or weather conditions that reflexively lead to corresponding changes in animal behavior. As the animal does not concern itself with symbols it is therefore forever trapped within his natural environment. It may, however, be trained to utilize man-made symbols as indicated in the classic Pavlovian experiments.[10]

The freedom of man lies therefore in the fact that not only does he utilize symbols—an attribute shared to some extent by animals of the natural world—but he alone invents and designs the symbols with which he is to transact. Symbol-using frees man to the extent that his pre-occupation with them allows him to turn his gaze from the physical environment that would otherwise incessantly impinge upon him.[11] He therefore receives inspiration and meaning from the artificiality of a flag or a game, and most fundamentally from language.

LANGUAGE

The meaning of symbols as epitomized by language is related neither to the instinctual natural make-up of man nor to the intrinsic properties of the symbol itself. As an instance, "livre" and "book" have the same meaning for the French and

English; the symbols obviously differ. Nevertheless, language is more than a pure abstract symbol such as a flag code or mathematical system. Experience is always inextricably woven into language.[12]

Language therefore is undoubtedly the cornerstone of man's symbolic world. It is through the use of language that we are able to transcend time and immerse ourselves in history so that we may communicate with people of another era. Through language we both store and communicate our experience with others in our world as well as that of our ancestors and in the world of the future.

Yet at the same time it must be recalled that not only does language free, it also binds man to a time, place, and what is most important, to a culture and civilization. It is language that nails man to his world nearly as unalterably as he is nailed to his very body. Language and with it a particular perspective and orientation is inevitably foisted upon man through the accident of his birth and circumstance. The language that he speaks therefore epitomizes the contingencies and circumstances—it is the embodiment of man's fictional nature—out of which he has been forced to forge his existence. Language and experience have been forcibly breathed into his very soul. It is this bondage that may give man his freedom.

Although man's experience arising from his situations as a child (as we shall see in the next chapter) may not be of his choice, as an adult he nevertheless is responsible for the misery and misfortune that it may bring to bear upon him. This condition is perhaps nowhere better epitomized than in the situation of the black man who must confront the language of the dominant white man. The predicament takes one of two forms: first, the black man is scorned for speaking what Fanon refers to as "pidgin" or the fact that he speaks the white man's language either poorly or well is made note of and thus a sense of humiliation brought to bear upon him.[13]

What I am asserting is that the European has a fixed concept of the Negro, and there is nothing more exasperating than to be asked: How long have you been in France? You speak French so well.

It can be argued that people say this because many Negroes speak pidgin. But that would be too easy. You are on a train and you ask another passenger: "I beg your pardon, sir, would you mind telling me where the dining care is?"

"Sure, fella. You go out door, see, go corridor, you go straight, go one car, go two car, go three car, you there."

No, speaking pidgin-nigger closes off the black man; it perpetuates a state of conflict in which the white man injects the black with extremely dangerous foreign bodies. [P. 35-36]

To speak a language is to take on a world, a culture. The Antilles Negro who wants to be white will be the whiter as he gains greater mastery of the cultural tool that language is. Rather more than a year ago in Lyon, I remember, in a lecture I had drawn a parallel between Negro and European poetry, and a French acquaintance told me enthusiastically, "At bottom you are a white man." The fact that I had been able to investigate so interesting a problem through the white man's language gave me honorary citizenship. [P. 38]

Some other facts are worth a certain amount of attention: for example, Charles-Andre introducing Aime Cesaire as "A Negro poet with a university degree," or again, quite simply, the expression, "a great black poet."

These ready-made phrases, which seem in a common-sense way to fill a need—for Aime Cesaire is really black and a poet— have hidden a subtlety, a permanent rub. I know nothing of Jean Paulhan except that he writes very interesting books; I have no idea how old Roger Caillois is, since the only evidence I have of his existence are the books of his that streak across my horizon. And let no one accuse me of affective allergies; what I am trying to say is that there is no reason why Andre Breton should say of Cesaire, "Here is a black man who handles the French language as no white man today can." [P. 39]

Second and perhaps most damning for the black is that at best to incorporate the white man's language is to sabotage his very self-image. How else can it be in a language where "white is clean," and "dirt is black"? Thus what the black man is led to believe makes it impossible for him to live in equanimity.

Language and symbol that ought to free instead oppress, enslave, and humiliate. What are the origins of the situation of man that allows for symbols and language to be the condition of his freedom as well as that of his enslavement?

THE OEDIPAL SITUATION[14, 15]

 *Chapter 3*

FROM ANIMAL TO MAN

The Oedipal situation can be said to be the prototype of the human situation in which man's drama of oppression has its inception. It revolves about the arduous trials that the child must undergo in order that he be converted from animal to human existence. It is within the Oedipal situation that the child is confronted with nothing less than the necessity to begin the mastery of life itself. This is in contrast to the narrower conception of the Oedipal complex as defined by the classical psychoanalytic schools which focuses more exclusively on the vicissitudes of instinctual drives that, as shall be indicated below, I consider to be mere artifacts or by-products of the human situation.

The core dimension of the Oedipal event, as I wish it to be understood, is centered on the complex and intricate transitional phase that characterizes the child's conversion from a biological creature to a symbolic actor. During this phase he must be transformed from a carefree instinctual creature to a careful social actor. In view of man's feeble instinctual make-up—in comparison to that of his animal brethren—not only must he develop an independent mode of existence, but one in accordance with both a social timetable and a setting, if he is to survive. From suckling he learns to drink, from being fed he must learn to eat; these steps are taken within a framework of a particular time and place peculiar to one's culture and circumstance. At one extreme, for the child who is later to become schizophrenic these steps may be painful and humiliating as he associates suckling and being fed with his being responsible for harsh demands to which he has subjected his mother. The child of a religious family may relate mealtime to the exhilaration of being provided bread by God and it becomes a joyful experience. It is in this manner that the natural instinctual endowments of a child are capped with specific symbolic meaning.

The paucity of the child's instinctual endowment is responsible for his helplessness that extends over a prolonged period. It is his helplessness that makes it imperative that he strive to obtain acclaim from others through mastery of their symbolic world. It is the child's period of extended helplessness on one hand that provides the impetus for his striving to become human and on the other makes it possible for him to so readily forfeit his manhood. It is no wonder therefore that this difficult transitional period is inevitably associated with enormous frustration and hardship that may only be overcome if the child is provided with a firm sense of general well-being. He incessantly seeks to receive both acclaim and affection by which he is better able to tolerate the inevitable hardships and frustrations that accompany him on his road to social mastery.

INCEST TABOO

How are we to relate the concept of incest with the events of the Oedipal situation as we have defined it? The incest taboo is synonomous with an element of restriction and repression that is invoked against the growing child in *all* known societies. The incest taboo signals limitations and restrictions that are placed upon the relationship of the child and the adults within his immediate circle.

In other words, there is no known society that tolerates or permits the male child to indulge himself in complete physiological or sexual gratification vis à vis all women with whom he is in contact. The Oedipal transition thus hinges on some form of incest taboo in that the conversion of a child from a creature of nature to a symbolic actor cannot be accomplished without the imposition of some restrictions on the child's physiological-natural urges. The limitations placed on the extent of physiological gratification to be enjoyed by the child become itself symbolic of the discipline that must be instilled into the child if he is to become a member of his social order.

It becomes clear, therefore, why no known people regard all women as mates.[16] A form of restriction must exist in that it allows for the necessary curbs to be placed on the child consistent with the needs of all social orders. Both attention and repression are therefore instrumental if the child is to resolve the difficulties of the Oedipal stage.

There are, however, variations among societies and cultures as to the roles of women within the inner circle of the child and consequently with the kind of relations called for between male child and his maternal figures. The focus of the incest taboo in so far as it signals the curbing of the physiological gratification may be on the mother in one society, on the aunt in another. The variations within the Oedipal situation and corresponding incest restrictions suggest that they have less to do with unalterable biological drives and more to do with the design and requirements of the particular social order.

THE CHILD AS PUPPET

The child in the throes of the Oedipal situation is asked to curb his instinctual propensities. As he gives up his instinctual physiological inclinations he is obliged to seek other guidelines and direction by which he is able to gauge his conduct and actions. He must resort subsequently to the task of modeling his actions and thereby base his identity on those adult figures within his immediate circle. The task is accomplished as he incorporates the symbolic communications directed to him and transforms them into cues for self-animation. He takes, in short, the attitude of the Other[17] toward himself.

> The individual experiences himself as such, not directly, but only indirectly, from the particular standpoints of other individual members of the same social group, or from the generalized standpoint of the social group as a whole to which he belongs. For he enters his own experience as a self or individual, not directly or immediately, not by becoming a subject to himself, but only in so far as he first becomes an object to himself just as other individuals are objects to him or in his experience; and he becomes an object to himself only by taking the attitudes of other individuals toward himself within a social environment or context of experience and behavior in which both he and they are involved.
>
> The importance of what we term "communication" lies in the fact that it provides a form of behavior in which the organism or the individual may become an object to himself. It is that sort of communication which we have been discussing—not communication in the sense of the cluck of the hen to the chickens, or the bark of a wolf to the pack, or the lowing of a cow, but communication in the sense of significant symbols, communication which is directed not only to others but also to the individual himself. So far as that type of communication is a part of behavior it at least introduces a self. Of course, one may hear without listening; one may see things that he does not realize; do things that he is not really aware of. But it is where one does respond to that which he addressed to another and where that response of his own becomes a part of his conduct, where he not only hears himself but responds to himself, talks and replies to himself as truly as the other person replies to him, that we have behavior in which the individuals become objects to themselves. [P. 215–216]

Although man may be conceptualized as one who is free and unique he must begin his existence by making himself out of the "stuff" of another.

> In fact, the world still seems to be inhabited by savages stupid enough to see reincarnated ancestors in their newborn

children. Weapons and jewelry belonging to the dead men are waved under the infant's nose; if he makes a movement there is a great shout—Grandfather has come back to life. This "old man" will suckle, dirty his straw and bear the ancestral name; survivors of his ancient generation will enjoy seeing their comrade of hunts and battles wave his tiny limbs and bawl; as soon as he can speak they will inculcate recollections of the deceased. A severe training will "restore" his former character, they will remind him that "he" was wrathful, cruel or magnanimous, and he will be convinced of it despite all experience to the contrary. What barbarism! Take a living child, sew him up in a dead man's skin, and he will stifle in such senile childhood with no occupation save to reproduce the avuncular gestures, with no hope save to poison future childhoods after his own death. No wonder, after that if he speaks of himself with the greatest precautions, half under his breath, often in the third person; this miserable creature is well aware that he is his own grandfather. These backward aborigines can be found in the Figi Islands, in Tahiti, in New Guinea, in Vienna, in Paris, in Rome, in New York—wherever there are men. They are called parents. Long before our birth, even before we are conceived, our parents have decided who we will be.[18]

It is as such that the contingent world about the child is gradually incorporated as his very own. To put it bluntly, the child is thus unavoidably brainwashed or duped; he may only hope that at best the world he has made into his own does not contain the seeds of his later undoing. If this not be the case, the child and later the man may, in becoming aware of the particular restrictive contingencies of his existence, free himself from them. As we shall see, the task in psychotherapy lies in this direction.

The family, in that it is able to provide the affection and sense of well-being so necessary to the child, is ideally suited to serve as the transmission belt by which the ideals, values, and contents of a culture are instilled into the child. The child's physiological self becomes incidental to the cultural self which slowly begins to emerge. Continual resort to wholly instinctual-type gratifications—homosexuality, alcoholism, and so forth—represent, as will be indicated below, the failure of the family to have provided the attention and sense of well-being so necessary if more fruitful modes of action are to be undertaken.

The meaning of this transitional process has, I believe, to a degree escaped the clinical acumen of some psychoanalytic workers. As such, the stages of childhood development heretofore taken for granted as fixed biological landmarks must be reinterpreted and understood as cultural artifacts rather than as naturalistic propensities. The focus of the child is not principally determined by natural libidinous processes but rather by the emphasis placed on bodily zones by the culture and family in its efforts to socialize the child. The oral and anal phases must be thus viewed as the techniques or means rather than as ends by which the child differentiates himself from the adult mother figure[19] principally to earn the acceptance of these potentially oppressive people.

Fromm's description of the receptive-exploitative, hoarding, and marketing characterological types represents his attempt to portray the influence of the social order rather than instinct in the formation of man's modes of being.[20] The modes of oral or anal behavior reflect the requirements and conventions of a particular society rather than the necessities of natural processes. Further, the extent to which these modes later remain as a way of life reflects the human condition within the particular social order. The latent phase described by analytic workers is in actuality a cultural artifact rather than simply a product of nature. The vehemence with which one side supports the "deterministic" perspective while the other its cultural approach illustrates the forcefulness with which man believes in his fictions. It may yet overtake even those themselves devoted to the uncovering of man's illusions.

INSTINCT VERSUS PURPOSE

How are we to reconcile our fictional view of man with that of the psychoanalytic viewpoint? The latter emphasizes man's inherent mechanistic instinctual nature; the former from a humanistic perspective considers man's physical endowment as peripheral rather than central. The question to be posed is whether man's instinctual nature is an unalterable fact as psychoanalysts would contend or is it a mere artifact of a particular human situation? It is the latter contention that is to be developed as a basic theme throughout this work.

It must be realized that the Oedipal situation with all its far-reaching ramifications is basically one in which the helpless child confronts the all-powerful oppressive world of adult figures. It is helplessness and sensitivity to the Other, as has been mentioned, that is a prime condition of human culture. The child is thus obliged to make himself into the person that the more powerful adults expect him to be. His concept of himself is a reflection of the attitude of the Other toward him; he is therefore obliged to take on the characteristics of the person he is to become in an unreflecting automatic fashion. For the moment he remains oblivious to the possibility that the attitudes and ideals which he has taken as his own may not at all be consistent with the needs of the man whom he envisions himself to be tomorrow. His present concept of self, designed to satisfy the demands of the Other, is often at odds with the exigencies of his own future existence. All this is to suggest that the Oedipal situation is basically a power struggle rather than one of sexual rivalry[21] between parent and child. The child as the weaker of the adversaries must often suffer unfortunate consequences in spite of the well-intentioned actions of the parents.

Human conduct as documented and described in the classical psychoanalytic studies must be interpreted within the context of this redefinition of the Oedipal situation. Psychoanalysis has mistakenly emphasized instinctual naturalistic components of the Oedipal complex abstracted from the power struggles that characterize the human situation.

The alternative is to reinterpret the vast and detailed clinical data meticulously gathered by the psychoanalyst through the years, in the light of our perspective as to the significance of the Oedipal situation and its impact on the child. It is characterized by the aforementioned power struggle as well as the many other obstacles and hardships that lie across the path of the child during this transitional period. It would not be at all surprising for the child prompted by either parental oppressiveness or protectiveness to attempt to evade the harshness of such social realities by losing himself in what may appear to be instinctual conduct or Oedipal gratifications. It is in this vein that Adler has written:

> The Oedipus complex is not a fundamental fact but is simply a vicious unnatural result of maternal overindulgence.[22]

All human conduct may therefore be considered to be an answer to the situation, past or present, that man has experienced. A mother fixation complex is not necessarily a derivative of natural instinctual drives but a device designed to extricate the individual from the harsh realities of his existence. One's preoccupation with oral and anal modes of existence is not an outcome of inherently fixated libido but provide gratification for the receptive or exploitive character who sees broader avenues of existence as beyond his reach.[23] I have therefore suggested some arguments in favor of interpreting instinctual-like phenomena as purposeful rather than naturalistic. Human conduct considered as purposeful obliges us to confront the wide realities of our existence. It necessitates close scrutiny of the totality of the human situation, knowledge of which is essential if we are rightly to understand the broad meaning of human conduct.

CULTURAL IMPOSITION

The Oedipal situation signifies the process by which man is socialized and thereby imbued with a way of life conducive to the working of the social order in which he lives. As an integral aspect of his ways, man develops a sense of awareness[24] and responsibility consistent with it. His awareness allows him to conceptualize a past, present, and future that provide him with a sense of continuity so necessary to his identity. It is during this process that there is implanted within man at least a modicum of individuality without which society cannot function. Nevertheless, it is also true as suggested above that the development of awareness and responsibility is unreflective and automatic as a result of the severity and intensity of the socialization process. After all, the child in his predicament must blindly develop a sense of self based on the dictates of his cultural order. It is perhaps this unfortunate development that has led to the well-known saying that it is man's tragedy to have been a child. Simply put, this means that the impact of the Oedipal situation is such that the values and ideals obtained and embedded during childhood often impede man's potential towards complete self-realization. His need to submit as a child often remains with him throughout adulthood and often clashes with his potential to become a free and responsible individual.

Free man thus begins his life by the forfeiture of his freedom. The task of life is perhaps nothing less than for man to recoup the power and freedom that he was forced to cede as the price he has had to pay to become a man. It is unfortunate that in its broad meaning, few people are able to resolve their "Oedipus complex." To the contrary, most remain in a stage of "immediacy" [25] unable to free themselves from the constricting effects of the values and ideals that their culture has foisted upon them. In short, most are unable to become the locus of autonomous meaning.

Psychoanalytic theory based on man as an unalterable, naturally endowed, instinctual animal is necessarily more deeply pessimistic in its outlook. It views man's bondage as an outcome of inherent antisocial instinctual drives for which cultural repression becomes a necessity if civilization is to survive. It therefore has little faith that the creative forces of history may foster the liberation of man. This pessimism may only be disproved if biological drives are to be considered in terms of man's sociohistorical situation. Such a reinterpretation would entail the envisioning of man and his drives not at all as a product of nature but rather as an invention of history.[26] Such a view allows us to reject pessimistic explanations of human conduct solely on the basis of man's biological nature, and rather consider man's biological or instinctual conduct as itself in need of explanation. The full significance, therefore, of the Oedipal situation as outlined herein is to emphasize that anatomy in fact does not represent the crux of man's destiny.

The anatomical configuration of an individual however does often become a cue that segments of the social order may very well exploit in its effort to limit the possibilities and opportunities that might otherwise be available to him. As an example, the psychoanalytic notion of the so called "penis envy" of women must not be taken literally to mean that the plight of women is reducible to their anatomical structure. Rather it is by virtue of their anatomical configuration that they have often been confined to an oppressive socioeconomic status. Women may, therefore, suffer from the effects of cultural imposition rather than on account of their bodily characteristics.

Throughout history, those with distinctive physical characteristics are often victimized and stigmatized through prejudice, myth, and a various assortment of lies. Stereotypic renditions of group characteristics are maliciously invented and anchored to anatomical particularities in order that they seem more convincing. The sensuality of the Negro, that supposedly exudes from his skin or hair, is an example of such a prejudicial myth attributed to a group's physical characteristics. Similarly, one cannot understand the plight of the child of a minority group nor, as we shall see, that of the neurotic as simply an outcome of biological circumstance (Oedipus complex). We must persistently concern ourselves with the entire range of the oppressive situation in which the child finds himself. In this light, our portrayal of the Oedipal situation suggests that emphasis be placed on its significance as a human situation through which all humans must pass rather than as a biological happening abstracted from social reality. To this extent man suffers on account of what others have made of him rather than by what he has made of himself.

THE SELF

--- *Chapter 4*

FACEMANSHIP

A central paradox of man is that the comparative strength and certainty of his body is offset by the relative flimsiness and tenuousness of his sense of self and pride. The vitality of his body has been provided as a product of nature with its ironclad laws of cyclical regularity designed to insure the survival of the species; man has not been quite so fortunate in regard to his sense of self-esteem. His sense of self is man-made and thereby subject to the whims, fancy, and caprice of others as well as himself. As a child, man is forced to develop a sense of self-esteem out of the attitude that the other has towards him, obviously a most precarious affair. The child who later becomes man now has within him the physical prowess to insure his biological survival; no longer helpless, he ought to have the possibility and capacity to—in a word—diminish the oppressive influence of the Other. That this task is not easily accomplished is attested to by our pseudoindividualistic age characterized by the "cheerful robots" or "outer directed" mass man.

In any case, it is clear that the source and origins of self-esteem lie necessarily beyond the bounds of the natural order.

One's self-esteem depends for little on the proper functioning of bodily and instinctual processes. It lies rather in the meaning and values given to man in his transaction with his symbolic world. Where one derives satisfaction from physical character-istics such as color or his line of ancestry, it is principally an outcome of social status and prestige rather than the inherent quality of the physical trait. In addition, there are limitless roles and performances by which a society can instill a sense of well-being in its members. Basically, however, the social fiction bestows its blessing on those willing to perform according to the prevailing dictates of social convention and values.

Our contemporary affluent society does much to emphasize the artificiality and tenuousness of man's self-esteem. It would appear that such self-esteem has little to do with either the at-tainment of pure physical comfort or for the matter with the development of somewhat more vague spiritual satisfactions. Rather, as an instance, terms such as "conspicuous consump-tion," [27] "conspicuous leisure," and "pecuniary emulation" have been coined by Veblen to describe the means, manner, and significance by which a cultural order artificially establishes its own criteria for self-esteem maintenance.

> The end of acquisition and accumulation is conventionally held to be the consumption of the goods accumulated—whether it is consumption directly by the owner of the goods or by the household attached to him and for this purpose identified with him in theory. This is at least felt to be the economically legiti-mate end of acquisition, which alone it is incumbent on the theory to take account of. Such consumption may of course be conceived to serve the consumer's physical wants—his physical comfort—or his so-called higher wants—spiritual, aesthetic, in-tellectual, or what not; the latter class of wants being served indirectly by an expenditure of goods, after the fashion familiar to all economic readers.
>
> But it is only when taken in a sense far removed from its naive meaning that consumption of goods can be said to afford the incentive from which accumulation invariably proceeds. The motive that lies at the root of ownership is emulation; and the same motive of emulation continues active in the further devel-

opment of the institutions to which it has given rise and in the development of all those features of the social structure which this institution of ownership touches. The possession of wealth confers honor; it is an invidious distinction. Nothing equally cogent can be said for the consumption of goods, nor for any other conceivable incentive to acquisition, and especially not for any incentive to the accumulation of wealth.

It is of course not to be overlooked that in a community where nearly all goods are private property the necessity of earning a livelihood is a powerful and ever-present incentive for the poorer members of the community. The need of subsistence and of an increase of physical comfort may for a time be the dominant motive of acquisition for those classes who are habitually employed at manual labor, whose subsistence is on a precarious footing, who possess little and ordinarily accumulate little; but it will appear in the course of the discussion that even in the case of these impecunious classes the predominance of the motive of physical want is not so decided as has at times been assumed. On the other hand, so far as regards those members and classes of the community who are chiefly concerned in the accumulation of wealth, the incentive of subsistence or of physical comfort never plays a considerable part. Ownership began and grew into a human institution on grounds unrelated to the subsistence minimum. The dominant incentive was from the outset the invidious distinction attaching to wealth, and, save temporarily and by exception, no other motive has usurped the primacy at any later stage of the development. [P. 35]

This fetishism of superfluous commodities illustrates not only the fictional nature of man's self-esteem but the facility with which life's expectations may be perverted by the demands of the market. It is the tenuousness of man's self-image that prompts him to reduce life's meaning to the owning of commodities through which he wins acclaim and respectability as well as gaining power over others. In this regard the importance of the Oedipal situation lies in that it provides the child with the awareness that no task or endeavor may be accomplished on his part without paying heed to the opinion and approval of the Other. The child learns that all his actions must be linked to a means of securing appraisal or validation. The more idiosyncratic "fetishistic" neurotic practices, yet ones having similar meaning, will be described in a later section.

Furthermore, the foundation of conscience is equally a precipitate of the Oedipal situation. It begins with the child's need to save his face—to insure his survival by placating the powerful adults in his world. It is therefore within this transitional period that the child must inevitably pay attention to all his actions. He learns that he will not be able to act unless he thinks well of himself. And to think well of himself he must maintain the acclaim of his parents and social order to which he belongs. The necessity for man to think well of himself (conscience) will always remain with him. The most heinous of criminals may need to be showered with approval for the loving care given to his family. He has the possibility, however, to alter the criteria by which he judges his actions and on which he bases his self-esteem. Psychotherapy, in fact, becomes the means by which the patient learns to convert from an unfavorable set of "self" criteria to one more conducive to his own interest.

The early criteria by which a child develops a sense of pride is based automatically on the actions that bring forth the approval of his parents. He gains their approval by adhering to the rules and prescriptions set down by society and thereupon transmitted to the child by his family. He must in one fashion or another adhere to these rules if he is to provide not only himself—but perhaps ever more crucial—the adults within his circle with a sense of self-esteem without which family interaction collapses. He maintains his face to a large extent only through preserving the face and dignity of the Other.

In all societies the child is not only taught to perform efficiently in a technological sense but at the same time he must protect the self-esteem of the Other as well as his own. The need to maintain self-esteem, although a prime motivation for human conduct, is a tenuous affair and as much a gamble as life itself. In order that this gamble be minimized and that a measure of security and order be provided to the members of society during the course of their daily interaction, all social actors must become experienced in the business of "impression management." [28]

> A performer who is disciplined, dramaturgically speaking, is someone who remembers his part and does it. He is someone with discretion; he does not give the show away by involuntarily disclosing its secrets. He is someone with "presence of mind" who can cover up on the spur of the moment for inappropriate behavior on the part of his teammates, while all the time maintaining the impression that he is merely playing his part. And if a disruption of the performance cannot be avoided or concealed, the disciplined performer will be prepared to offer a plausible reason for discounting the disruptive event, a joking manner to remove its importance or deep apology and self-abasement to reinstate those held responsible for it. The disciplined performer is also someone with "self-control." He can suppress his emotional response to his private problems, to his teammates when they make mistakes, and to the audience when they induce untoward affection or hostility in him. And he can stop himself from laughing about matters which are defined as serious and stop himself from taking seriously matters defined as humorous. In other words, he can suppress his spontaneous feelings in order to give the appearance of sticking to the affective line, the expressive status quo, established by his team's performance, for a display of proscribed affect may not only lead to improper disclosures and offense to the working consensus but may also implicitly extend to the audience the status of team member. And the disciplined performer is someone with sufficient poise to move from private places of informality to public ones of varying degrees of formality, without allowing such changes to confuse him. [P. 216–217]

Tact, courtesy, and salutations are the common everyday ingredients necessary for the maintenance and development of a sense of self-esteem. As would be expected, the task of maintaining self-esteem is necessarily compounded in more densely populated areas of the world. Under such conditions one's self-esteem is more susceptible to the confrontation and scrutiny of the Other. Elaborate rituals of courtesy and salutation have therefore been developed specifically to protect and maintain the self-esteem of the populace.

DISCONTINUITIES IN SELF-ESTEEM

I have suggested that man cannot act unless he attaches meaning to his action. It is therefore one's experience of himself and his possibilities for action within a situation that becomes the mainspring of human action. As meaning is inevitably linked to the concept of one's self, it behooves us now to inquire into the ramifications of man's necessity to derive his self-esteem from the actions he has undertaken.

The concept of self-esteem is, as already indicated, first developed within the confines of the family situation. The family is best able to provide the self-esteem necessary in order that the child tolerate the inevitable frustrations that ensue as he strives to convert himself from an erotic or biological creature into a social actor. The child learns and never forgets that henceforth all his actions must be woven into a pattern of meaning inherently related to his self-concept.

The psychotherapist in his practice is witness to the discontinuities and inconsistencies in the modes by which man must maintain and derive his self-esteem. These discontinuities come to the fore as the expectations placed upon the child by the family are often in marked contrast to the duties he must fulfill as he becomes a member of adult society. The child who is encouraged to be weak and powerless learns to derive a sense of satisfaction from his very helplessness. The demands of life make it impossible that he continue to derive satisfaction in the face of his state of powerlessness; yet all too often he knows no other way. He is forced to persist in his ways of helplessness, aided and abetted by his neurotic tactics. Neuroses, as I shall indicate in more detail, are an outcome of the paradox in which the child, to protect the face of those oppressive figures within his immediate circle as well as his own, must forfeit both his executive powers and experience of autonomy. As he has been required to exaggerate the sacrifice of such experience and power, he no longer remains able to cope with the demands of existence. He is therefore forced to exploit his state of weakness wherein lies the entire meaning of neuroses. The intensity and bizarreness of neurotic symptoms are thereby a reflection of the depth to which man has descended through the experience of unreflective powerless ways designed only to maintain his self-esteem at the price of giving himself up to the dictates of others and eventually to the realities of existence.

It is perhaps worth noting a possible converse situation, namely one in which consistency is achieved in the maintenance of self-esteem during the period of both childhood and adulthood. One would expect consistency between childhood expectations and adult demands to exist as a real possibility. Nevertheless, the existence of such consistency by itself often does not suffice to provide its members with a satisfactory sense of pride, virtue, and accomplishment. This may perhaps best be illustrated by Fromm's marketing character[29]—one who forfeits his powers as a child and continues to "sell himself" as an adult. The sacrifice of power, individuality, and vitality begun in childhood continues throughout adulthood as the means by which one maintains his adjustment to the demands of society.

It is perhaps the violence and chaos of modern times that is a consequence of the shallowness and flimsiness of the self-esteem of the man of today. For the marketing character who symbolizes the man of our time, self-esteem is unfortunately based on a fundamental but perhaps unwitting tactic of powerlessness. The need to resort to violence on a collective basis becomes a means of bolstering and solidifying the ensuing sunken self-esteem of the masses. The masses suffering from a constricted and humiliated sense of pride are forced to turn to violence as a source of more satisfying action. In such circumstances the indulgence in violence becomes a refuge from the imminent anxieties of life in the same way that the neurotic symptoms protect the individual from his sense of overall powerlessness. The marketing character exemplifies what Fromm has referred to as the "pathology of normalcy." As such it should not be at all surprising that in many aspects both the neurotic and mass man of our day mint their self-esteem from the very same metal.

CONCEPTS OF ANXIETY

The concept of anxiety is closely linked with that of self-esteem in that anxiety signals man's failure to maintain an adequate sense of self. Self-esteem is in its origins a measure of whether or not the child is skilled at conforming to the social fiction transmitted to him via his family milieu. If the child fails in this effort or is unwilling to fulfill the expectations of the social fiction, he is threatened by the displeasure of the parent and is beset by unavoidable anxiety. This anxiety signals and recalls to him that his very survival depends on whether or not he fulfills social expectations. Anxiety, therefore, for the child, is an outcome of his inability or refusal to partake in the social fiction and thereby to invite the disapprobation of his elders.

In this regard the various well-known defense mechanisms of repression, introjection, conversion, and sublimation become in effect tactics that the youngster devises for himself in order that he better conform to parental expectation or at least give the appearance of doing so. The inclination to avoid school, for instance, is converted into stomach pains whereby the child is able to fulfill his wish to remain at home and yet not incur the wrath of his parents.

It cannot be stressed often enough that once again the child is naturally unaware of the high cost to himself of having had to avoid oppression and anxiety through limiting his behavioral experience. As he conforms to social and parental expectations it is true that he may minimize his anxiety but only at the price of a loss of experience and power. As an adult—to the extent that he has compromised his powers and is no longer in a position to receive parental solace—he will be all the more unprepared to face the later exigencies placed upon him by fundamental existential demands.

Neurotic anxiety in its variety of designs and tactics may be said to provide at least a semblance of refuge from the ever-present fundamental existential anxieties of life. Similarly the social order, in its "fetishisizing" of success, in its emphasis on the acquisition of commodities, screens one from the more basic existential question of success for what? Goods for what?

ROLE-PLAYING AND IDENTITY

A major task of society is to assure a measure of order and predictability that allows its members to function with the minimum of anxiety. Each society creates for itself particular rules that govern individual enactment of a multitude of assigned roles which in turn provide order, predictability, and self-esteem for all concerned. The functioning of all institutional orders necessitates the prescription and enactment of roles based on a hierarchy of status. Man by means of his performances gains approval and a sense of satisfaction for himself as he provides dependability and order to the Other. Status and role-playing are inseparable aspects of man's rule-following propensities.[30] Status and role enable us to write prescriptions for human action that have the effect of minimizing anxiety for the individual as he obtains a sense of worth by providing predictability, order, and meaning for society at large.

In one's role as a waiter or a physician the infinite possibilities of human action become narrowed to fit the requirements of the social context. The anxiety of the unfamiliar and unexpected is allayed as one fulfills the prescriptions of his role and status. As each performer enacts his role within the definition of the situation, he accrues a sense of identity that helps to define a situation in which a minimum of anxiety prevails.

Historically in the life of the individual the establishment of roles and rules are the means whereby the child is pried out of his original dyadic-erotic physiological relation with his mother and into the social world. The future adult, in complying with the rules required of him in the enactment of his varied roles, is provided with responsibility, meaning, direction, and satisfaction so that he is able to tolerate the frustration and anxiety that is otherwise an inevitable accompaniment of the process of de-differentiating[31] himself from the mother figure. Infantile attachments lose their significance as the child is edged into becoming involved and concomitantly receives satisfaction from the more challenging roles delegated to him as he seeks to attain manhood. Conversely, with the lack of available roles positive identity formation is stifled, which in turn heightens primitive infantile anxieties and logically calls for a more concerted attempt to secure extensive physiological gratification.

The overindulgence in physiological gratification that persists beyond childhood signals the fact that important symbolic possibilities have not been seized upon. It must be clear that the achievement of physiological gratification is not synonymous with what it means to be a man but merely incidental to it. To the degree that one accrues a sense of identity in confronting the tasks and complexities of life, physiological concerns become peripheral. Drug addiction or alcoholism may be seen as attempts to by-pass the difficult chore of securing symbolic satisfaction.

Natural physiological maturation is necessary but not sufficient to enable one to forge a creditable sense of identity. The child does not become man in the way the tadpole becomes a frog. Nor does he first become a man with poise and confidence and then a man who is a politician, a carpenter, or a physician. Skills, talents, and poise are developed neither as an outcome of natural processes nor in any abstract fashion prior to the enactment of one's role. It is the experience accrued in having enacted one's role that remains crucial. One becomes what he does.[32] Man is what he makes of himself rather than a simple happening of nature.

PROBLEMS IN IDENTITY FORMATION

I learn that I must strive to *become* as it is not possible for me to remain what I have been. I have been obliged to forfeit the tranquility of the womb; it has thereupon been necessary for me to forego the pleasures of being cuddled and fondled. I am forced to relinquish the familiarity of my relation with my mother—to embark on other more varied complex and unfamiliar tasks. I am thrust into the world to enact roles and conform to rules that have been already selected for me.

Although many possibilities await my beckoning, there are at the same time hurdles, obstacles, and impediments that I must overcome in my attempt to become myself—to find out who I am and where I belong. As things are, however, I often find myself in a situation in which you attempt to bolster your pride and prestige by coaxing me to forfeit mine. I have become unwilling to act without manifesting concern for you. You regard it as your right that I be at all times concerned with you. My possibilities to act are contingent upon your approval. It is a simple task to imagine how easily my possibilities and my potential are thwarted and restricted by the sense of obligation and guilt imposed upon me by you. It is this perverse condition and accentuated by the tenor of our times (Chapter 6) that permeates human relationships to the extent in which I am forced to retreat from my sense of being in order that I enhance your own. I am left with only a sense of powerlessness and resentment that emanates from the impositions placed upon me. This predicament is poignantly portrayed by Kafka:[33]

This little woman, then, is very ill-pleased with me, she always finds something objectionable in me, I am always doing the wrong thing to her, I annoy her at every step; if a life could be cut into the smallest of small pieces and every scrap of it could be separately assessed, every scrap of my life would certainly be an offense to her. I have often wondered why I am such an offense to her; it may be that everything about me outrages her sense of beauty, her feeling for justice, her habits, her traditions, her hopes, there are such completely incompatible natures, but why does that upset her so much? [P. 235]

So the only thing left for me to do would be to change myself in time, before the world could intervene, just sufficiently to lessen the little woman's rancor, not to wean her from it altogether, which is unthinkable. And indeed I have often asked myself if I am so pleased with my present self as to be unwilling to change it, and whether I could not attempt some changes in myself, even although I should be doing so not because I found them needful but merely to propitiate the little woman. And I have honestly tried, taking some trouble and care, it even did me good, it was almost a diversion; some changes resulted which were visible a long way off, I did not need to draw her attention

to them, she perceives all that kind of thing much sooner than I
do, she can even perceive by my expression beforehand what I
have in mind; but no success crowned my efforts. How could it
possibly do so? Her objection to me, as I am now aware, is a
fundamental one; nothing can remove it, not even the removal
of myself; if she heard that I had committed suicide she would
fall into transports of rage.[P. 239]

As an outcome of my role of powerlessness which you have
demanded of me my potential and possibilities of existence are
often denied. I have been encrusted in an armor plate fitted
snugly on me by you. My talents and capabilities I have cast
aside in an effort to avoid any confrontation with you. I have
seen no other alternative but to be forced into the role of weakness and helplessness from which the pattern of my future neurotic conduct is to emerge. The myriad of neurotic symptoms
that have slowly become a part of my being serve to solidify
my retreat and withdrawal from your grasp. I hide my talents
and refrain from the exercise of my capabilities as I have come
to believe that I have neither the right to be heard nor to act.
My ensuing weakness makes it certain that in order to survive I
must beg and appeal to you rather than rely on the belief and
strength of my unique performance. It is nonetheless my remaining pride that I attempt to bolster as well as to conceal the
weakness that prompts my resort to neurotic symptoms.

If the situation were yet more drastic I would look to create
a more intense and idiosyncratic reality wherein by way of my
psychotic roles my retreat would be yet more final. Yes, you
have judged me harshly and condemned me mercilessly. It is
only within the safety of my psychoses that I may express my
being or lack of being and yet be spared your overpowering
presence so inimical to my very person. There is yet another
possibility; I may turn to crime or violence. The violence I have
learned so well as I have observed you in your ceaseless act of
inflicting it upon me—violence to which I must now resort
in order to preserve a morsel of pride in the face of my retreat
from all else.

The obstacles and discontinuities that face man on the road

to becoming himself are thus difficulties encountered at the level of self, family, and society. The basic and most obvious discontinuity that exists within man in all societies is that the child must become father. What appear to be discontinuities of nature through which all men must make their way—birth, puberty and death—are not at all comparable to the natural process by which the caterpillar metamorphoses into the butterfly. Within the human order these natural phenomena are enmeshed and fitted into the institutional framework of the particular social fiction. The institutional frameworks through which the child must pass on his road to becoming a man vary from culture to culture as well as from civilization to civilization.

Our modern Western mobile industrial society is characterized by a plethora of roles and vocations amongst which I must choose. In part, the difficulties and confusion in identity formation stem from what seemingly is a choice of roles. The plethora of available roles is part of the confusion that is consistent with the breakup of traditional values and beliefs that have heretofore sustained man in the exercise of his freedom to choose. When the traditional bonds of association—family, community and church that have provided man with his self value—have been ruptured, the prospect of freedom and choice, and together with it the forging of identity, become more ominous.

By contrast, let me briefly mention the more traditional society of the primitive. It is characterized by a paucity of roles on one hand, as well as a traditional and highly institutionalized framework on the other, that is more conducive to the establishment of a sense of identity. Long-established roles and status provide for more certainty in man's quest for a sense of identity than in a highly mobile, forward-looking society. Further, the natural discontinuities and anxieties of birth, puberty, and death are more easily offset by the ritual dramas that make more secure and satisfying these transitional phases through which all men must pass. The traditional, more stable framework of the primitive thus minimizes confusion as well as limiting the kinds of pernicious all-pervasive competitive characteristics of contemporary society. Study of the primitive traditional societies reveals to us the often elusive notion that reality is infinite. It is neither possible nor necessary that we copy their social order but simply to realize that aspects of our social structure which we take for granted provide merely one possibility. Our social structure is our particular historical creation rather than our unalterable destiny.

THE OUTCAST

The difficulties of forging an identity are further compounded for one stigmatized [34] by virtue of his skin color, a physical anomaly, or particular ancestry. It is ostensibly on this account that he becomes imprisoned in a role that has been emptied of all hope. The limitations placed upon one who is stigmatized are such that within the confines of his role he is unable to forge a positive sense of identity no matter what his skill or effort. He is damned by virtue of what he is; what he does matters little.

The harshness of the reality imposed upon him by the stultifying values of his society is all too acutely sensed by the stigmatized. He experiences severe oppression and this accounts for the accompanying despair, apathy, or rage on his part. Conversely, the exuberance and joy of one whose status is changed from an "out" to an "in" group is thereby easily understood. The stigmatized, therefore, suffers not from a confusion of identity but rather from the fact that he is all too keenly aware of the condition in which he finds himself.

It is not the inherent nature of his skin color, ancestry, or physical characteristic that is responsible in any way for the deformation of his person. It is rather a reflection of the culturally imposed ideas that are affixed to these characteristics that lead to his debasement. The limitations imposed upon him as well as the degradations he has suffered are not fortuitous happenings. They are meant to enhance the identity and prestige of his oppressors. As such

I would call anti-Semitism a poor man's snobbery . . . by treating the Jew as an inferior and pernicious being I affirm at the same time that I belong to the elite.[35]

The stigmatization of the Negro forces him to dream of being white. He dreams of becoming white as he cannot find dignity in his blackness. Too often, to remain black is to allow one's life to be stolen. He therefore believes that in adopting the ways of the white man he will attain the dignity and pride that he should otherwise be obliged to forfeit. In this quest he fails to realize that in his effort to escape his blackness he will not at all appease a culture whose self-image rests on a persistent need to manifest its superiority. The parallel between the plight of the neurotic and that of the stigmatized is all too obvious and will be further dwelt upon below.

FUNDAMENTALS OF EXISTENCE

-- *Chapter 5*

The reality of my identity must be forged out of the varied modes of my existence. The elements of human existence have heretofore been sketched rather abstractly; I now propose to consider further dimensions crucial to the task of comprehending the events relevant to the emergence of the human individual.

SOCIAL CONTEXT

As human existence is neither accidental, isolated, nor meaningless, it takes its origin within the confines of a social situation. It is not at all akin to the movements of the planets within their orbits—all in keeping with the iron laws of the natural world—or to the interactions that occur between electronic or planetary systems. Human interaction involves far more than the confrontation of bodies. It involves the confrontation of bodies impregnated with experience[36]—experience in having lived life. The human experience is one based on fears, plans, and hopes that one has about his life. It is an awareness and consideration of experience that make human interaction meaningful in contrast to physical bodies that interact as a pure happening according to the plan of nature.

My action or inaction is not of a mechanistic stimulus–response order; rather it is a reply or question in keeping with the realities of my interpretation of the world. More than that, it is an expression of my experience of having lived in the world. My plan of action thus reflects both experience and awareness.

I must be more precise; my action reflects my experience of the world, of space and time, of today and tomorrow. The time and space of my world demand that I act within it and in no other. My action has relevance only in terms of the situation which prevails upon me. My action moves me toward or away from the situation as I experience it. It is the situation—my experience within it—that remains the central clue to the meaning of my action. I may protest that my dedication to truth and justice are time-worn absolute values that must be the only considerations upon which my action rests. My interest in incorporating such absolute values into my actions is authentic to the extent that I have taken the reality of my current situation into account. In other terms not only time but place is crucial.

Human action must unavoidably be woven from the strands of the social setting in which it takes place. Psychoanalysis, in one of its dimensions, has painstakingly depicted the experience and conscience of the child as an outcome of the contingencies of his social circumstance. It has, however, at the next moment reversed itself in postulating the presence of deep-seated unconscious impulses and drives, innate to man, which supposedly serve as the springboard for his action. As such, it has attempted to discount the importance of situations, social context, and the political–economical conditions in which such drives are enacted, manifested, and expressed. It seems to have forgotten the lesson it has taught; namely, that human action becomes intelligible if the situation in which it occurs is uncovered, revealed, and thereupon correlated with the experience of the actor.

It must be recalled that to the extent to which we accept explanations of human action reducible to terms of either constitutional-organic traits, affective disorders, or so-called intrapsychic conflicts we inadvertently minimize the relevance of the social situation. How then are we to consider the problem of affects or intrapsychic conflicts? Simply, they must be explained on the basis of the social context in which they occur. If man is yet to be understood by the science of psychiatry and furthermore if such comprehension is to lead to the liberation of man, we must persist in our pursuit of a thorough exploration of the social origins of man's nature. It is when we understand man as a social actor who is trapped within a labyrinth of institutional forces that we become aware of the means and facility with which values and experience are foisted upon him. In this light, we must further seek to expose both the conditions and values of a society that have remained as impediments to man's liberation. It is, after all, the values and experience instilled within him rather than any libidinal fixations that have made man what he is.

DECISION AND DEED

It is perhaps true that the possibilities and meaning of both my actions and my deeds take on their significance principally in light of their social context. Nevertheless, in maximizing social responsibility we must take care lest we minimize individual prerogatives. We must not totally abandon the existential dictum that it remains our prerogative to be free to choose even in the most drastic of situations in which we find ourselves. Allen B. Wheelis, in *The Desert*, writes:

> Look at the wretched people huddled in line for the gas chambers at Auschwitz. If they do anything other than move on quietly, they will be clubbed down. Where is freedom? . . . But wait, Go back in time, enter the actual event, the very moment; they are thin and weak, and they smell; hear the weary shuffling steps, the anguished catch of breath, the clutch of hand. Enter now the head of one hunched and limping man. The line moves slowly; a few yards ahead begin the steps down. He sees the sign; someone whispers "showers," but he knows what happens here. He is struggling with a choice: to shout "Comrades! They will kill you! Run!"—or to say nothing. This option, in the few moments remaining, is his whole life. If he

shouts he dies now, painfully; if he moves on silently he dies but minutes later. Looking back on him in time and memory, we find the moment poignant but the freedom negligible. It makes no difference in that situation, his election of daring or of inhibition. Both are futile, without consequence. History sees no freedom for him, notes only constraint, labels him victim. But in the consciousness of that one man it makes great difference whether or not he experiences the choice. For if he knows the constraint and nothing else, if he thinks "Nothing is possible," then he is living his necessity; but if, perceiving the constraint, he turns from it to a choice between two possible courses of action, then—however he chooses—he is living his freedom. This commitment to freedom may extend to the last breath." [P. 94] [37]

As we shall see, the plight of the neurotic lies in that man suffers severely when he cedes his rights of decision; his hope is that the options within his situation are not as desperate as that of the inmates of Auschwitz. We cannot recoil from decisions in the belief that circumstances are beyond our control. What appears to be necessity may upon closer scrutiny reveal itself to be merely a possibility. As Wheelis expressed it in *The Desert:*

The realm of necessity, therefore, must comprise two categories; the subjective or arbitrary, and the objective or mandatory. Mandatory necessity—like natural law which cannot be disobeyed—is that which cannot be suspended. It derives from forces, conditions, events which lie beyond the self, not subject to choice, unyielding to will and effort. "I wish I had blue eyes," ". . . wish I were twenty again," ". . . wish I could fly," ". . . wish I lived in the court of the Sun King." Such wishes are irrelevant, choice is inoperative; the necessity impartially constrains. And since it cannot be put aside there's not much arguing about it. "If you jump you will fall, whether or not you choose to fly." There is consensus, we don't dwell on it, we accept.

Arbitrary necessity derives from forces within the personality, but construed to be outside. The force may be either impulse or prohibition: "I didn't want to drink, but couldn't help it." That is to say, the impulse to drink does not lie within the "I." The "I," which is of course the locus of choice, does not "want" to drink, would choose otherwise, but is overwhelmed by alien force. "I want to marry you," a woman says to her lover, "want it more than anything in the world. But I can't divorce my husband. He couldn't take it . . . would break down. He depends on me. It would kill him." Here it is loyalty, caring for another's welfare, which is alleged to lie outside the deciding "I," which therefore cannot choose, cannot do what it "wants," but is held to an alien course. As though she were saying, "I do not here preside over internal conflict, do not listen to contending claims within myself to arrive finally at an anguished, fallible decision, but am coerced by mandates beyond my jurisdiction; I yield to necessity." The issue is not one of conscious versus unconscious. The contending forces are both conscious. The issue is the boundary of the self, the limits of the "I." [P. 88] 38

It must be remembered that passivity, retreat, and abandonment are in themselves a decision for which we are held accountable:

To live is to feel ourselves fatally obliged to exercise our liberty, to decide what we are going to be in this world. Not for a single moment is our activity of decision allowed to rest. Even when in desperation we abandon ourselves to whatever may happen, we have decided not to decide.39

To believe conveniently but erroneously that it is, for example, the law and not men who kill is in reality a "decision not to decide." It is therefore a decision to deny our subjectivity in favor of accentuating our passivity. Such a decision is tantamount to the falsifying of our being in the interest of inaction; we are all too often unaware of the self-humiliation and degradation to which it will ultimately lead; the misery of neurosis ought to signal to us the price of such falsification.

When I react rather than act, when I disengage myself rather than become engaged, it only serves to falsify and distort reality. The truth toward which one must strive can only be envisioned by taking upon oneself the risk of confrontation with the world of man and nature.40 The authenticity of knowledge can neither be established by the criteria of our state of mind nor by insight to our feelings. The accuracy of my knowledge concerning my being depends on my actions in the world.

To know the truth, in a word, means that it must be practiced, lived, and experienced.

To strive for truth involves me in the necessity to act and decide freely in spite of the risks involved. It is my only possibility of becoming myself; it is the way to the truth. The dilemma of the neurotic is that he acts hesitatingly and conditionally as he seeks to avoid the risks of deciding freely and thereby forfeits the possibility of becoming himself. We have a stake in believing that man may strive for truth in his actions. If we are to be consistent we must attempt to refute the prevalent notion that our freedom is curtailed by, for example, what appears to be the necessity of our state of mind, emotions, or past memories. For if our actions were thus curtailed the quest for truth, freedom, choice, and decision would be meaningless. It is freedom not necessity that limits our freedom.

MIND AND EMOTION: CAUSE OR CONSEQUENCE?

If we are to believe that man may choose and decide, he must have the freedom to create reality for himself. He will never accomplish this task if we are to saddle him with a conglomeration of excuses and alibis that hamper his efforts. The causal deterministic approach to human conduct unfortunately provides in its body of theory precisely this manner of excuse that man so often desperately seeks to foster his inclination in the direction of limiting his freedom. This approach, inherent to the modern technological age, is manifest by a predominant contemporary psychiatric theory that explains deviant behavior such as mental illness as an outcome of a disorder of either mind or affect or both. This basic notion which in effect implies that man is victimized by inner forces has, in addition, sociopolitical ramifications upon which I shall later elaborate.

Let me first dwell on the issue of the "mind." I shall suggest that the state of the mind is neither the cause of rational human conduct (as already implied) nor of mental illness but rather mirrors them both. Human action, decision, thought, and imaginings are not the product of secret internal causes[41] but more properly must be construed as the workings of my mind. My actions and thoughts refer not to internal causes but to the world as I experience it; they reflect the choices that I may consider to be my possibility within the context of the social setting. The workings of my mind are therefore unavoidably enmeshed within the fabric of social and political meanings.

Human conduct postulated in terms of causes—an outcome of internal "ghostly" sensations—must necessarily exclude the supposition of man's action and mind as reflecting available choices within the sociohistorical situation as the principal dimension of human conduct. Human action explained on the basis of causality such as disorderly impulses of the mind tends to suggest that such conduct is a type of naturalistic mechanistic meaningless happening. Happenings cannot involve us in the issue of motives, purposes, alternatives, and intentions and are therefore beyond the realm of human freedom and decision. Human actions viewed by this naturalistic light take on the spectra of meaningless events that follow the haphazard law of nature.

If we are to eschew explanations of human conduct in terms of causal agents such as the mind, how then are we to conceptualize man's conduct? In an effort to construct a rational humanistic framework by which we may interpret human conduct, let us consider the words of Ryle:[42]

> My performance has a special procedure or manner not special antecedents.

Our comprehension of human action is therefore to be based on our concern with the rules, procedures, and consequences of our daily actions. It is in our inquiry into the rules and tactics to which man adheres that allows us to clarify the meaning of his actions. The distinction between rational and irrational conduct cannot be made by the postulation of the presence of causal-impulsive factors in the case of the latter and their absence in the case of the former. Rather, what appears to be irrational conduct is merely that conduct based on rules, values, and beliefs unfamiliar to the observer. It is the idiosyncratic obscure rules that the neurotic follows in maintaining his self-esteem that make it difficult to comprehend his behavior rather than the presence of any "deep-seated" internal derangement or disorder.

If I am to characterize myself as ambitious or vain I need not postulate the existence of hidden impulses, sensations, or processes within my mind that determine such conduct. Rather, in concluding that I am either ambitious or vain I must analyze, observe, compare, and study my actions, mannerisms, and attitudes toward my work and other people.[43] It is my inclination or disposition to follow a set of rules; namely, to boast before others that allows for the analysis and categorization of my conduct as one who is vain. Any claim on my part to the effect that my conduct is an outcome of causal impulses, if we are to adhere to our framework, must be challenged. I may well feel "impulse ridden" but only to justify my disposition to act in a particular way. In a similar vein, if I were to imagine or picture during some spare moments the Eiffel Tower that I had visited last summer, I do not do so by invoking vague sensations of the tower in my mind. I am not observing or picturing a resemblance of the tower; rather in my imaginings I merely resemble an observer of the tower.[44] It is therefore through my disposition and tactics of conduct rather than through the presence of any sensation within the mind that I imagine the tower.

Human action and thought (a type of action) presupposes dispositions, inclinations, and rules rather than the postulation of sensations within the mind. The sensation or impulse, if one exists, is always an outcome or consequence of my disposition toward a particular action. The workings of the mind are therefore not at all to be studied in the experimental laboratory or within bodily processes but on the stage of life where rules and procedures are daily enacted and encountered.

EMOTIONS, AFFECTS AND INSTINCTS

The principal contemporary psychiatric conception of human conduct, and mental illness in particular, is that it is caused by the presence of repressed or aberrant emotions, affect, and instincts. I submit that this contention has severely undermined the notion of individual volition as well as the concepts of spontaneity of action and therefore the prerogative to decide and choose for the following reasons: First, such a theory is both an outcome as well as a support to a cause-effect model of human behavior of the kind where supposedly repressed affect, as an instance, leads to mental pathology, aberrant conduct, and so forth. A theory steeped in terms of causality as mentioned accounts for human action basically in mechanistic terms that are beyond individual control and isolated from the context of the human situation based on the existence of both purpose and meaning. A theory of causality is therefore antithetical to the exigencies of the human situation that revolves about the elements of spontaneity and subjectivity. Second, man is viewed as one who is naturally endowed with antisocial, irrational, brutish emotions that tend to deny his potential for responsible action. Third, emotions are considered to be essentially intangible, ephemeral, and somewhat mysterious phenomena that operate beyond the limits of concrete existence, responsibility, and reason.

It is undoubtedly a truism that various expressions of emotions, affect, and feelings such as depression, guilt, and fear are cardinal manifestations of human conduct in general and in their more intense form are part of the mental illness syndrome. It is on the basis of this display of emotion that we commonly declare a man to be irresponsible—to be overwhelmed by instinctual, naturally endowed forces beyond his control. Rather than explaining human conduct, do not such biomechanistic interpretations of man's actions simply serve to justify the needs and tenor of our technological era? Is such postulating not consistent with the modern inclination to consider individual option as subordinate to political and industrial collectivistic interests that are geared to technology, efficiency, and rationality and therefore often at odds with the concept of uniqueness, spontaneity, and choice?

How are we then to interpret the phenomenon of emotions and affects so that it is consistent with a humanistic framework that takes into full consideration the dimension of spontaneity, responsibility, and purpose? We must suggest that what has been understood as explanation of human action in fact needs further explanation itself. In this vein the manifestation of emotion and impulsivity is not at all a causal naturalistic happening that operates beyond the control of the patient. Rather, further inquiry reveals such expressions to possess meaning, uses, and consequences that are an indication of man's very ability to respond to anticipated danger and failure by acting as if he were either passive and helpless on one hand, irresponsible and impulsive on the other. In short, his intense emotions become the means whereby he may act as if he were a *thing*. It is at times man's exaggerated guilt, depression, fearfulness, and anger that he at one and the same time both creates and seizes upon in an effort to persist in his goal of passivity. It is therefore neither the constellation nor intensity of emotions that explains human conduct; to the contrary, these very emotions are the expressions, manifestation, and consequence of the oppressive human condition that prompts man to shrink from responsible, reasonable action.

Consistent with a humanistic framework, Adler insisted that the emotions and instincts which Freud took to be "cause" were in fact "consequence." The former described heightened emotions, feelings, impulses, and instincts as artifacts created by the individual. The intent, in this instance, was to provide himself with excuses or alibis so that he could continue to maintain his life plan geared towards retreat and withdrawal from the demands of existence. He has written:[45]

> The affects are not mysterious phenomena which defy interpretation; they occur whenever they are appropriate to the given style of life and the pre-determined behavior pattern of the individual. Their purpose is to modify the situation of the individual in whom they occur, to his benefit. They are the accentuated, more vehement movements which occur in the individual who has foregone other mechanisms for achieving his purpose or has lost faith in any other possibilities of obtaining his goal.

His view allows for the conceptualization of emotion and instinct in terms consistent with the humanistic concept of originality, spontaneity, decision, and choice that is basic to man as a creative animal.

Sartre[46] in his phenomenological analysis of the problem of emotion lends support to these basic contentions. He states:

> . . . emotional behavior is not a disorder at all. It is an organized system of means aiming at an end. And this system is called upon to mask, substitute for, and reject behavior that one cannot or does not want to maintain. [P. 32]

Further, he comments in regard to a specific emotion:

> . . . sadness aims at eliminating the obligation to seek new ways, lacking the power and will to accomplish the act which he had been planning we behave in such a way that the universe no longer requires anything of us. [P. 65]

Emotions, affect, and feelings, therefore, are neither inborn naturalistic phenomena that lie beyond the realm of human meaning and volition nor are they instrumental in the causation of human conduct. To the contrary, they must be interpreted as purposeful creations designed to facilitate one's retreat from obligation and responsibility. As we shall see in the next chapter, it is in the situation of neurosis and psychosis where such withdrawal is most pronounced.

Such retreat is manifest on one hand by resort to violent impulsive behavior or on the other by conduct marked by passivity and inertia. An outcome of the contemporary psychiatric framework is that both these modes of conduct are thereby explained in terms of the natural endowment of the individual or group rather than as a reflection of man's historical situation.[47] *

---

* By contrast, Fanon offers an outstanding sociohistorical analysis regarding alternating episodes of violent and passive conduct in the Algerian native. According to Fanon the source of such conduct is not at all biological but is to be interpreted on the basis of the oppressive and coercive social setting.

THE PAST

Tomorrow and Yesterday

Man thus conceptualizes his mind and emotions as mechanisms that control, hamper, and restrict his actions. He is too often inclined to recall an overbearing past that he is convinced equally hampers his actions of today. Is this not equally a matter of self-deception by which he seeks to recoil from his freedom that inevitably points him to the future—to the day beyond today?

Life is a task and a struggle that inevitably, willingly or not, presupposes a plan of action. Human action based on purpose, motive, and reason implies that I must inevitably look beyond today. Man cannot but move forward. Conditions of existence do not permit man to make time the captive he has made of space. He must inevitably, though often reluctantly, shrink from what he has been; the movements of time make this inescapable. Time is a prime mover of men. It is therefore primarily my projects and goals of tomorrow rather than my experience of yesterday that are central to my action of today. My very aimlessness of today may in itself be a plan designed to cope with the pessimism with which I envision the future. It is paradoxically the clandestine goal and orientation of the neurotic that by remaining what he always has been, he will cope best with the future—which sheds light on what otherwise strikes us as bizarre conduct.

Although man is propelled inevitably toward his future he nevertheless maintains the possibility of looking toward it with either pessimism or hope. In general, if my goals and visions lie beyond the realm of simply satisfying his immediate self-centered necessities, today and tomorrow have the possibility of becoming more meaningful. To have a goal beyond myself implies that I have the potential to fit my life into a framework that boldly transcends the immediacies and necessities of my proper existence; I may thus better cope with my anguish of tomorrow. If this possibility is excluded, as with the neurotic, my life becomes an end unto itself and inevitably turns about itself. As is too often the case, I become ensnared anxiously in an endless labyrinth of apparently purposeless movement so characteristic of our day. I am therefore tempted to seek a past consistent with my pessimism of today—one in which my chances have been limited and, what is more important, a gloomy past which both engulfs and looms large so that I may conveniently look away from the disappointments of today.

CREATION OF THE PAST

My past is thus arbitrarily created and selected in accordance with my conduct of today and my intentions of tomorrow. I manipulate my history purposely to lend continuity to my actions of today and tomorrow.[48] I look to yesterday to support my goal of tomorrow. Tomorrow's meaning is bolstered by the manner in which I manufacture my past. It is man's awareness as to the fictionality and fragility of his identity that demands that he establish a semblance of continuity through which he may link his past, present, and future actions. He thus is able to fortify his sense of identity and self-esteem in forging a degree of unity out of all the moments of his days.

My intention to become an athlete is bolstered by my yearning for the bygone days spent on the ball field. If I now posit a new goal or project for the future, it then will become very likely that I look at my past in a new light. I now instead decide to complete my college education; I seek out past experience to justify such action. I now become aware of the yesterdays, spent not on the ball field, but recall vividly the delightful hours engaged in browsing through the world of books.

It is not only my future that shapes my past, however. It is my probing into the past that solidifies, illuminates, and clarifies my goals of tomorrow. My goal for tomorrow prompts my selective interpretation of my past and in turn my past modifies and qualifies the goals and projects of my choice. Further, I study my past basically in an attempt to escape its limitations. It is my actions of today and yesterday that must inevitably fall short of my expectations. As no man may dare affirm that he has accomplished all that he ought to have done, I therefore look to yesterday to ascertain the manner and method by which I have veered from the fulfillment of the tasks set before me. I understand and investigate my ways of yesterday in order to fulfill and carry out with more integrity the task of today and tomorrow. History, both individual and social, is inevitably an endless road of failure, not success. It is the tactic of the neurotic who in seeking to perpetuate his retreat clings tenaciously to his past in order that he not meet up with the awareness that it perhaps be discarded for a new one pointing to a more courageous future.

PAST AS AN EXCUSE

My past implies possibility for future action rather than unalterable destiny:

> It stands behind me like a boneless phantom. It depends on me alone to lend it flesh.[49]

An event or fact of my past as any other cannot exist independent of my interpretation. It has been said that a fact is like a sack that will not stand up unless something has been put into it.[50] I therefore choose my past in light of my future intentions. I thus fill the empty sack of my past with factual events that support my projects of today and tomorrow. As an example, the homosexual looks to the fact of his fair skin and light hair that he claims have made him unalterably into what he has become and that he unknowingly wishes to be. He remains unaware that his preoccupation with the delicate features of his youth is not the cause but the consequence of his need to bolster the meaning of his homosexual pursuits. He recollects features of his past in order that he persevere all the more steadfastly in his conduct of today. The very same facts of his youth could have been utilized to support his determination to excel as an athlete or establish himself as a family man. Such physical features could easily have provided him with a uniqueness that he would have preferred to maximize and exploit to his advantage. In other terms the facts of his past reflect his intentions of today.

If we are inclined to view man as a passive object, a strategy that often justifies oppression, we are likely to consider him to be controlled and manipulated by his past, his mind, and emotions, as the supposed "cause" of his actions. On the other hand, if man is to be considered free, his past, mind, and emotions must be seen in the light of the very creativity of his freedom; the state of his mind, emotions, and past are consistent with his purposes, intentions, and projects.

THE PROBLEM OF MEANING

Life demands that I act and through my actions I inescapably reveal myself to the world and become aware of who I am. Through all my actions, in spite of my freedom, I cannot avoid either implicitly or explicitly answering the one fundamental question—what is the meaning of my life? In what do I believe? For what shall I strive and in what manner? For what am I needed?

As our mode of existence reflects possibility rather than necessity, we are entitled to speak of man's inability to do without choosing; choice is inherently linked to meaning. To speak of meaning is not possible if man could not decide freely. Happenings in the world of nature are meaningless or at least beyond human comprehension. To consider the presence of human meaning in life is to suggest the possibility and perhaps even ironically the necessity of spontaneity, subjectivity, and creativity. Man by virtue of his freedom—freedom from the ironclad necessities of nature—stands not only within but beyond the cycles of nature and is thereby able to choose his meaning. Meaning in its fullest dimension joins man's view of himself, the world, and God into a coherent framework with which his actions are henceforth consistent.

As I cannot but choose, I must become inevitably involved in a choice of meaning. Meaning, devotion, and belief are both peculiar and necessary to man in contrast to other creatures. The final choice of meaning for either the individual or the nation may be understood as necessarily one between good and evil; ultimacy and immediacy; God and idolatry. Man may choose to anchor his meaning in either his fragile finite self or in a cause beyond that of self or nation. Belief and meaning devoted wholly to one's self or self-surrogates characterizes the state of neurosis as well as that of sin (Chapter 8).

The neurotic position stands as a continual reminder of the fact that man's mind is a factory that ceaselessly and unhaltingly manufactures meaning. If in this regard classical religion is principally a framework of meaning, then neurosis may be viewed as an idiosyncratic self-styled religion. The issue that ensues is not whether man must believe—this is unavoidable. But rather, what are the origins, significance and consequences of his meaning framework; of what worth is that in which he believes?

I now proceed to an analysis of neurosis as one variety of man's inescapable quest for meaning and belief that may serve as a paradigm by which we can judge and weigh all our actions. Inevitably we shall have to conclude that neurosis indicates man's inability to do without meaning and yet at the same time how his beliefs and consequent action may undermine his very existence. In spite of the sterility and fruitlessness of neurotic meaning, it nevertheless will remain with him until his life situation permits him to adopt other more ennobling convictions.

NEUROSIS IN SOCIETY AND MAN

--- *Chapter* 6

A primary task of this chapter is to suggest a means or format by which the problems of the individual may be linked to the texture of the society in which they originate (as well as to the fabric of life itself—the subject to be developed in Chapter 8). As part of this overall effort I shall attempt to suggest an interpretation of neurotic conduct—a principal form of personal problem—as a microcosmal portrayal, or, if you will, as an artifact that reflects social movements, forces, and trends of the day.

As an example of the impact of social forces on human conduct it has been suggested that sexual behavior described in the famous Kinsey Report is not about human males but about American men in the twentieth century.[51] Similarly, what we call "woman" is not a product of nature but rather an invention of history. In a similar vein I shall submit that neurotic or so-called irrational conduct is less a matter of instinct and more a consequence of the individual's position within a particular sociohistorical situation. This would imply that neurotic conduct is a particular response to the demands of a specific sociohistorical situation rather than a behavioral phenomenon merely accidental to the human situation.

Neurotic conduct is then to be considered a human reply fitting to a particular social context rather than simply a naturalistic-accidental happening. The central purpose of this chapter is to suggest that neurosis is preeminently a human condition in which we become witness to the violence, oppression, and degradation inflicted on man by men and conversely on men by man. Within it I shall strive to demonstrate the interrelationship of individual and collective action through an analysis of fundamental neurotic patterns. We may then conclude that the existence itself of neurosis implicates the social structure as essential to both its origin and meaning.

In my effort to accomplish this task I shall present a tripartite interpretation of neurosis. The first and third parts will refer to the suprastructure and infrastructure respectively of the neurotic pattern. In the second part I shall describe neurotic tactics that link together the supra- and infrastructure of neurosis. However, prior to the portrayal of each of the segments of neurotic conduct, I shall present a description of the contemporary social circumstance in which I believe today's neurotic patterns have their origin and from which they derive much of their meaning.

I. NARROWED EXISTENCE

The idiosyncratic narrowed world of the neurotic is not the product of man's instinctual heritage but rather an invention designed to cope with the existing limitations of contemporary social reality. Constrictions and limitations exerted by the force of contemporary institutional forces serve to effectively narrow the scope of man's world. The neurotic stance that we shall witness is simply an exaggeration of the one in which modern man in general no longer originates or acts but merely reacts or adapts to an oppressive situation.[52] This narrowed posture of contemporary man reflects his social circumstance which in turn is an outcome of the contemporary existential predicament.

It is basic anguish over loss of this existential direction and meaning (Chapter 8) that prompts man to evade anxiety and fear of the unknown and eventually culminates in a situation as follows:

> War and the planning of war tend to turn anxiety into worry; perhaps as many seem to feel genuine peace would turn worry into anxiety. War making seems a hard technological and administrative matter, peace is a controversial and ambiguous political word. So instead of the unknown fear, the anxiety without end, some men of the higher circles prefer this simplification of the known catastrophe.[53]

Man's social world is transformed into the constricted world of worry, simplicity, and certainty, whereby he may avoid facing the acute loss of existential meaning and purpose. What are the consequences of this quest for a narrowed simplified world?

This contemporary quest is characterized by a felt need for certainty, simplicity, and uniformity; it is undoubtedly associated with the concomitant rise of centralization and bureaucracy that has become woven into the fabric of modern life. We are witness to the creation of a collectivistic technological society undergirded by a functional elite who head large anonymous centralized governments and associated industrial complexes. The overall outcome is the disappearance of the multifunctional, multievaluational person who embodies the spirit of community life. The nucleus for group solidarity is no longer the community but becomes rather "fragmented publics" headed by the typical but narrowed, technically efficient organization man. Society as a whole becomes a microcosmic portrayal of a situation in which people no longer know each other in a diversity of roles but only on a selective basis as they interact in a fragmentary fashion. The potential for diversity is thereby reduced. Life tends to become narrowed to the extent that it may be said that in effect we live in a substitutive culture where bonds, checks, notes, degrees, certificates, and so forth, displace the essence of human experience.[54] The outcome is the fetishization of technology, the principal faith left to man and with which he must now sustain himself.

I might mention at this point that collectivistic appeal to

supposed universal aims is in reality a desperate attempt to overcome the ill effects of such narrowing by providing a semblance of direction and meaning through slogans and promises of progress, peace, and unity. Such an appeal may tend to offset the deep sense of insignificance in those who have given their allegiance to the institutions of which the social order is composed. The collective suprastructure thus attempts to provide meaning to sustain the way of life of its members (see this chapter, Part III), as the neurotic symptom provides meaning and purpose in accordance with the mode of existence of its bearer.

What is of concern for the moment, however, are some of the means by which man unwittingly reduces his own world and at the same time enhances and augments the power, functioning, and authority of these centralized collectives. In this vein Mills has further written:

> Christian morals are now used as moral cloaks of expedient interests rather than as ways of morally uncloaking such interests.[55]

This phenomenon is part and parcel of the modern era in which we are witness to the disappearance of the small associative group such as the family, guild, and church in the linkage between the individual and the state. These associative groups have been rendered impotent as their functions are no longer in step with the functions of the larger state or the general goals of our economy. On one hand the virtues of family life are extolled and on the other the family often proves a handicap for a man striving to get ahead in the business world.[56]

We find ourselves in a situation in which we ostensibly opt for freedom, choice, and individuality but at the same time mercilessly strip away the very supports that are necessary to nurture freedom:

> The assumptions of philosophies of freedom have been that freedom lies within the individual himself. . . . We now see that these traits were abstracted from social organizations (family, church and guild) that actually give rise to autonomy . . .

individuality is most tolerable when the basic elements of social organization are present.[57]

In the name of humanism, release from constraints of traditions has been exaggerated and individuals have progressively found themselves in a rarefied medium too difficult to endure. The result has been the filling in of the vacuum by the rapid growth of the large state and corporation that has progressively displaced the small associative group. And with it the forfeiture of man's ability to withstand the anguish of freedom and spontaneity in the face of the pressures placed upon him by collectivistic organizations.

The displacement of the family, church, and community—the narrowing of existence—is yet furthered as the political foot of the public is whittled down to fit the interests of the collectivistic shoe; as an instance, when congressional critics suggest that debate within Congress encompasses only the middle levels of governmental policy. If this be the case has not Congress, as representative of the people, abdicated its duly delegated task of advice and consent? It instead has been content to occupy itself with the more insignificant and trivial issues and thereby distract public opinion from more important issues. In its mere mirroring of the policies of the central arm of the government it allows the functional elite to create its own narrowed version of contemporary reality through the vast multifold power of its office.

We may thereby conclude that the radical realities of existence are no longer confronted; they have been replaced by artificial collectivistic suprastructures that in view of their expediency unavoidably narrow the existence of its members. I now proceed to illustrate how neurotic modes of existence are in essence the means by which the individual curtails his sphere of life the better to cope with these realities of his social circumstance.

II. NEUROTIC SUPRASTRUCTURE

It must be quite clear to all who are witness to neurotic conduct that it most obviously narrows the scope of the patient's
existence. This central fact is evident and observable prior to
any further or more penetrating analysis of the patient's symptoms. Neurotic symptoms, from this perspective, simply exclude the patient from the possibility of participating in
broader and more rewarding spheres of life. The question that
poses itself at this point is a crucial one. On one hand, is the
neurotic symptom—a natural phenomenon, merely accidental
to the human situation—a product of causes? Or on the other, is
neurotic conduct a human, purposeful, reply to a particular
crisis within a sociohistorical setting as just described? It is the
latter contention that I shall obviously attempt to support. I will
at the outset attempt to illuminate and clarify this contention by
way of contrasting Freudian and Adlerian views of the neurotic symptom.

Both Freud and Adler, in spite of their markedly divergent
views, envisioned the neurotic symptom as one that is basically
individual in its origin and significance. Both these pioneers of
modern psychiatry have in essence postulated theories of personality confined essentially to an individual framework.
Nevertheless, I shall contend that it is the philosophical framework espoused by Adler which is more fruitful in our effort to
link neurotic conduct with the particularities of the sociohistorical setting. By contrasts, the Freudian orientation has a defi-
nite deterministic, biological strand that often serves to obfus-
cate the social dimensions of man's conduct and I shall deal
with the ramifications of such a view in Chapter 7.

If Freud views man as a biological instinctual animal, Adler
to the contrary insists on his being basically a sociopolitical
creature. As such, for Adler the neurotic is defined as one who
loses himself in other than the sociopolitical arenas of life. He is
one who withdraws from a spirit of cooperation in which man
strives for the betterment of humanity. In this regard the symptom is the means by which the neurotic believes it necessary to

accommodate himself, not to his instinctual make-up but to that which he views as the oppressive demands of his life. The neurotic creates his symptom in order to enhance his withdrawal from the demands of an existence that he believes to be excessively harsh. His symptoms allow him to tread lightly and put his foot forward into the game of life only on a conditional basis.

He gives the impression that he would be a willing participant in this game of life "if" it were not for his disabling symptoms:

> The neurotic secures himself by retreat and secures his retreat by intensifying the symptoms.[58]

His symptoms therefore represent a maneuver in that at the same time that he seeks to withdraw from his responsibilities, he seeks favorable recognition and approval for his inaction.

The patient's preoccupation with an odor or with an excessive interest in cleaniness as in the situation of the psychotic or compulsive indicates in its most simple meaning his inclination to turn from the tasks of the day. Accuracy, punctuality, and orderliness in the compulsive become ends in themselves rather than the means to enhance one's productivity. The main battlefield of life is thereby eschewed as attention is focused on these newly created subsidiary concerns.

Further instances of such withdrawal are the substitutive actions and veiled communications expressed by the neurotic symptom. It is consistent with this perspective to interpret hysteria in terms of body language, cheating, or hinting.[59] Paralysis or dizziness, as the case may be, becomes "a way-out" yet permits the maintenance of self-esteem. Szasz, however, follows the traditional psychoanalytic explanation which suggests that faulty familial training in regard to excessive authoritarian influences rather than the forces of social circumstance have made these patterns of behavior expedient.

Becker,[60] to his credit, provides us with a broader perspective of the neurotic framework. In discussing the depressive syndrome as utilizing guilt language, he suggests that although self-defeating these communications are last-ditch efforts to preserve a shread of meaning, continuity, and control in the life of a person who has been beset by narrowed choices brought on by social circumstances. Such a person may be a middle-aged housewife whose children marry and leave and who is now bereft of both family and career finds herself unable to establish new meaningful objects. The self-accusatory language of her depressive state suggests that she sees herself as worthless or evil; this is in preference to the more drastic realization that for her life itself has no meaning. Guilt language thereby narrows the existence of the depressive in keeping with what he believes to be the narrowed realities of life.

Therefore, what appears to be irrational behavior such as an individual's preoccupation with guilt may be in fact an actual indication of the paucity of meaning possibilities within the cultural framework. The observation of a diminution of hysterical behavior in women in the wake of marked economic and social reforms that have improved their social status and prestige in the last several decades would lend credence to this postulation.

In this light the full meaning of the statement that

> Neurosis is a creative act and not a reversion to infantile and atavistic forms[61]

becomes apparent. Neurotic conduct may therein be understood as purposeful and spontaneous rather than as simple mechanistic phenomena. It is purposeful in that the symptom provides the patient with a measure of self-esteem that he is unable or unwilling to secure in the world at large.

III. THE OTHER AS ENEMY

It is the pervasive collectivism of our day as well as rampart individualism that is responsible for the narrowing and fragmentation of modern man's existence. He thus is unable to have the totality of his existence confirmed in either the individual or social dimensions of life. In both spheres of existence he becomes merely an object to be exploited.

This predicament is manifested in the social dimension by the absorption of the individual within the grasp of the all-embracing governmental or industrial collective. This development is both a consequence of as well as being fostered by the disappearance of the traditional associative group that previously instilled within the individual a sense of purpose, value, and meaning. These associative groups have now been replaced by the large centralized organizations that have permeated all spheres of life. The latter are necessarily distant as well as anonymous; as such, men are not able to obtain the ingredients from them so necessary for the growth of free rational and purposeful individuals. In such a setting men are easily transformed into publics consisting of atomized masses; it is this condition that fosters the replacement of freedom by power.

Man thus becomes truly a cog in a machine; an object to be exploited in accordance with the needs of the collective within which he is situated. He is used and manipulated; his value is dictated solely by the ends and goals of the collective. Man is converted from a person into a thing by institutional forces that conceal as well as rationalize most effectively its egoistic aims; far more effectively, I might add, than may be accomplished within the interpersonal or individual dimension.

The collective, by virtue of its size, anonymity, organization, and power, is able to confound its own base and egoistic aims with ostensible universal ends and thereby aggrandize its power and force of persuasion. It is able to cloak its base aims and pursue its egoistic interests under the guise of noble pursuits. Ideological and holy wars are prosecuted against a devilish enemy; slogans such as "protectors of the peace," "destroy to save," tend to become commonplace and justify the perpetuation of such conflict.

Modern-day giant collectives consisting of industrial, military, and governmental complexes are thereby able to provide a sense of purpose, meaning, and order to assuage the anxieties that accompany man's narrowed existence. Such meaning and purpose provides a most effective source of unity and cohesion wherein the masses are typically rallied in common cause against the Other who is declared to be the implacable enemy. Heightened anxieties that would otherwise arise are thereby mollified by the facility with which the collective may resort to means of violence and egoism under the cloak of benevolent universal aims.

The collective man must participate in or condone violence to offset the sense of insignificance now inherent in his situation. A vicious circle ensues in which violence breeds insecurity and insecurity breeds the violence in which man now looks for his meaning in the face of a narrowed world. Under such circumstances the "moral equivalent" of war and violence remains unsurpassable. Violence demands unity against the enemy and unity provides purpose and direction in a world whose meaning possibilities have been narrowed. It is within the individual dimension as well that meaning, purpose, and well-being are secured by means of exploitation of the Other. It is in the ordinary sadomasochistic relationship that this situation is revealed most prominently and to this I now turn.

IV. NEUROTIC TACTICS

The symptom of the neurotic is undoubtedly the means by which he tends to narrow the scope of his existence, an existence that mirrors the constricting realities of the social order. It is one in which the individual is confronted with a paucity of meaningful choices and, as a consequence, a limitation of available possibilities and opportunities. Neurotic symptoms therefore enable the patient to persist in, at the very least, a partial retreat from the unrewarding realities of his day. They are the means whereby his worldly commitment and human responsibilities are conditioned, qualified, and compromised. He regards the world with hesitancy; he conditions his mode of existence to coincide with what he views as the bleakness of his sociohistorical situation. He remains, in fact, by virtue of his abdication, compromise, and conditional commitments, a spectator to the significant events of his life.

However, no individual may thoroughly and completely avoid the tasks and decisions that are inherent in the human situation. Neurotic tactics in themselves represent a decision, albeit unwitting, of withdrawal. It remains, therefore, to investigate the meaning and consequence of this decision. What is the price exacted of one who decides to remain an aloof spectator to the significant issues of his life? If in fact his decisions and actions have little relevance to the central sphere of existence he must thereby seek a sense of value, purpose, and meaning through engagement in subsidiary activities. A narrow subsidiary existence, however, endangers one's sense of worth and value without which man cannot exist.

The disposition to retreat is furthered and compounded by the realities of social circumstance in which it has been said that "the more useful things man has the more useless he will become." I refer to the inimical forces of our modern technological age that have paradoxically reduced man's multifunctional capacities; as his potential for diversity is minimized the task of maintaining self-esteem becomes yet more precarious. In order that he quell the ensuing heightened sense of anxiety as well as redeem his sense of worth, the neurotic chooses, however, desperately to thrust himself upon those people and objects within his own immediate circle. Other modes of maintaining self-esteem within such a social setting are discussed in Chapter 8.

It now bcomes crystal clear that the neurotic symptom serves as a double-edged sword. On one hand it allows the neurotic to narrow both the individual and social spheres of his life and thereby facilitate his retreat. On the other it provides the neurotic with a means to maintain an ostensibly respectable status within his inner circle of associates from whom he must now derive a sense of self-esteem and worth. The precariousness of his situation makes it necessary that he obtain such self-esteem by resorting principally to tactics of power, coercion, and manipulation. It is either through submissive or domineering tactics that such power is secured. I shall describe these tactics as engaged in by masochistic and sadistic characters respectively, as I have encountered them during the course of psychotherapy and as such the individual and interpersonal rather than social dimensions are emphasized as in the case of Mrs. H.

Mrs. H. is a married woman of thirty-five with two young children whose initial complaints revolved about her increasing difficulty and fearfulness at having to remain at home alone in the evening. She is plagued by anxieties and fears that have to do with her husband's frequent business trips that make it necessary for him to be away from home. Yet another predominant complaint of Mrs. H. is her overwhelming anxiety at having to shop or to drive by herself; and if such was necessary she would be beset by dizziness, nausea, and giddiness. This state had progressed to the extent where she no longer felt able to carry out her chores without either the assistance or presence of her husband. Curiously enough, she maintains that this state of affairs began quite suddenly several years ago when while shopping by herself she recalled vividly the death of her father-in-law several days before. She is here basically attempting to portray her symptoms as accidental rather than directly linked to her way of life.

Her situation is designed so that it culminates in her virtual abdication and capitulation to her oppressive sadistic husband who now assumes full responsibility for the care of the household and all decisions involved in its maintenance. Contrary to her hopes, her abdication is met by callousness and aloofness on the part of her husband. At this point it is not too early to surmise that her complaints focus on the fact that her strategies of abdication and withdrawal have brought little in return. In other words, her capitulation rather than accidental was intended as a type of *coercive blackmail* wherein she virtually "ransoms" herself in return for care and acceptance on the part of her husband whom she maintains in the role of oppressor.

In order to justify her current actions Mrs. H. recounted her personal history in which she often sought to be pleasing by way of "blackmailing" others into having an appreciation of her. She cited the frequency with which as a child she often would give her candy to her friends. As an adult she slowly began to realize that such strategies were often futile, that in fact one was cheated and cheats oneself through such appeasement.

The theme of having been "cheated" was explored further as Mrs. H. became more aware that it was precisely her resentment toward her husband which she expressed by means of her irritability and bad moods that came upon her as he arrived home at the end of his day's work. This was in contrast to her relative tranquility and calmness during the day when she was on her own, yet could anticipate his arrival at the end of the day. Her moodiness was her way of signaling to her husband her distress at having received little or nothing in return for her abdication and capitulation. Her bad moods not only reflected her resentment toward her husband but disappointment in herself as well. Her withdrawal from responsibility accentuated her dependence on her husband's arrival at home and consequently her anguish as to whether or not he would accede to her requests that he assist her in driving and shopping.

As an aside, Mrs. H. often commented on her distaste for women who would shop by themselves, at times engage in flirtatious behavior and generally behave more spontaneously than she. Her dizziness then can be construed as a self-imposed means of restriction to avoid such temptations and consequent criticisms.

Mrs. H. brought up the subject of her pessimism in regard to what she believes to be the bleakness of her future. Once again, it would seem that it is pessimism about her person and capabilities that she accentuates in a coercive effort to secure care and interest from the next person. In her pursuit of her pessimistic ways she inadvertently and unwittingly yet realistically dampens her future prospects; she becomes what she believes herself to be. It is the price she must pay as long as she persists in her effort to gain protection, interest, and concern through the undermining of her own efforts while simultaneously aggrandizing the powers of others—in this instance principally that of her husband.

The ring closes yet tighter; her life possibilities narrow; so she becomes more convinced that her future is being stolen from her; she has little choice but to capitulate further. Her vision of her future was both the outcome as well as the reason for her perception of herself as having little power over her life; it concomitantly reflected her disappointment that her life given over to others has brought forth so little in return. In other terms she desires to reap the fruits without taking the trouble to sow the seeds or, put otherwise, she has sown the seeds in the garden of the Other rather than her own. Her disappointment and pessimism reflected her mistaken belief that to be a "patsy"—to allow herself to be exploited by the Other—did not necessarily mean that the favor would be reciprocated.

The many questions posed to me during our psychotherapy sessions in regard to matters such as the question as to whether or not she ought seek employment, whether or not she was progressing, what books she ought to read, and so forth may be construed as further efforts on her part to avoid at all costs a stance of decisiveness, a stance she has come to believe will alienate her interlocutor. Her dizziness in these terms can be simply conceptualized as her exaggerated effort to signal her feebleness and inclination literally to "disappear" from the possibility of confronting the Other.

The theme of capitulation as a *tactic toward the end of subtle coercion* is consistent with Mrs. H.'s apologetic and guilt-ridden stance whereby she finds herself either unable to decline, as an instance, invitations to affairs that she does not desire to attend or to refuse those people inclined to impose themselves upon her. In short the language of "no" remains as yet foreign to her. Instead, her prevailing hope is that in accommodating others she will in turn be accommodated herself. Her pessimism is in keeping with her inclination to abdicate, apologize, or withdraw. In this she is bolstered by her "near life-long addiction" to the game of bingo which she plays regularly and earnestly; it seems to offer her the hope that somehow a consolation prize will be bestowed upon her by the Other and perhaps redeem her life-long efforts of capitulation.

Along with the theme of guilt, obligation, and capitulation is Mrs. H.'s ever present fear of loneliness. Once again she banks on her mistaken notion that to avert the problem of loneliness she must enslave herself to the extent that she allows her husband to dictate and decide in regard to household and family concerns and in return she will be provided with meaning, order, and security by virtue of his presence.

Unaware of either the purpose or consequences of her solicitous behavior, Mrs. H. recounts the facts of her daily unhappiness in her own home; she cites as an instance her husband's tyranny in controlling programs to be watched on the family television set and her having little to say about the matter. Mrs. H. has stated that were she to persist in having her way her husband would threaten to leave her. Paradoxically, Mrs. H. does admit that in fact her husband would not leave. It becomes clear her fears of loneliness and rejection allows her once again to more steadfastly maintain her stance of capitulation.

It is outside the home as well that Mrs. H. remains plagued by fears. Her disappointments at home are compounded as her dizziness she believes does not make it possible for her to seek employment. Yet her dizziness must be understood as a consequence of her choosing not to seek employment. The meanings of this choice are multifold:

It is basically a tactic to coerce and intimidate Mr. H. toward treating her more benevolently by accentuating her weakness. Dizziness is therefore not the cause of her difficulties but her means of solving them. It is not difficult to envisage the many problems solved by dizziness such as the matter of friends imposing themselves upon her. Unwilling to say no to the Other she accomplishes this intent through her dizziness. Yet she unwittingly says no to herself as well. (I refer to the perpetual denial of her own powers and life's experience.)

We have thus far focused on Mrs. H.'s efforts to coerce and dominate through strategies of capitulation and apology. It is not at all surprising to take note of Mrs. H.'s contention that her husband resorts to similar tactics. He is inclined to flaunt his business setbacks, body ailments, and so forth, with sufficient vigor to maintain Mrs. H. in a role of capitulation. Mr. H.'s efforts are intensified to the extent that Mrs. H. attempts to demand rather than beg for her rights.

Curiously enough, we become aware that not only does the masochist or slave rely on the Other to maintain his status but such reliance is viewed as equally necessary by the master or sadist. Both slave and masochist as well as master and sadist are equally intimidated by the spontaneity and freedom of their interlocutor.

In summary, then, the typical masochistic, depressive, anxiety-ridden housewife is one who attempts to *seek power and status through her weakness.* She has sought to win by losing. In response to what she envisions as the harsh realities of her total existence she seeks to remain passive and withdrawn. She hopes to gain acceptance in order to abdicate responsibility by enticing her husband into treating her as an object or thing and therefore heeds all his commands and allows him to make any and all decisions. She becomes a servant in her own household; yet apparently believes that her self-imposed bondage will serve as a hint to her husband that he provide for all her needs and that in this fashion they will be best realized. It is by means of her ostensible devotion and submissiveness to her husband that she hopes to establish security, meaning, purpose, and order in her life. Further, it is by her own coercive tactics of helplessness and passivity that she clings to her husband and through him seeks to maintain her sense of worth. Her fears, anxieties, and phobias allow her to persist in this mode of submission.

The counterpart of this housewife is the sadistic compulsive husband who seeks power as an end in itself by means of his ceaseless domination, subjugation, and criticism of his wife. His tactics, in addition to those mentioned, are his compulsive belief in order, punctuality, and cleanliness which provide him with not only an apt distraction from the more significant tasks at hand; it furthermore becomes a pretense by which he may justify his critical domineering ways. It is in the practice and carrying out of his compulsive beliefs that he is able incessantly to undermine his wife's every attempt to manifest her individuality. As such her wishes become subject to his approval. He manages the household, family, and expenditures with an iron hand. He demands acquiescence and is unable to tolerate dissent. This form of "symbiotic union" is designed to shield him from a sense of powerlessness and fraility that would otherwise become more manifest. In the wake of the anguish of the problems of existence he demands subservience and conformity to his compulsive authoritative demands; he has no other means whereby he is able to maintain his much-needed sense of worth and righteousness.

To conclude, one could easily suspect that coercive tactics would most likely be fostered in a social structure, as described above, in which action possibilities are constricted and which thereby makes more tenuous the maintenance of self-esteem. Under such conditions power and coercive tactics become the sole means of providing purpose and security. One must be at all times aware of the social parameters that encourage and promote coercive or manipulative behavior; it is these tactics that form a core element of neurotic conduct. Only when we consider these social dimensions do we become fully cognizant of the inherent difficulties involved in relinquishing these strategies. We may well speculate that in the patients who seek our assistance their extremely lowered sense of value necessitates the use of more drastic strategies of power than is usually the case. Symptoms are thus often well-disguised techniques to engage in power plays. Disguise or concealment is necessary as the exercise power is less easily contested and therefore tends to be more compelling.

V. THE NEGATION OF FREEDOM

I have indicated that there is a marked correlation between the narrowing of existence in the individual (as exemplified by neurotic conduct) and social spheres of life. As a consequence, we find ourselves in a situation in which man has allowed himself to become objectified; he has converted himself from a person into a thing in a frantic effort to maintain meaning and order in the face of a crisis wherein he has lost his overall direction. This predicament may be more lucidly grasped by focusing our attention on the paradoxes that lie within as well as characterize both social and individual modes of existence.

The central meaning of a state is simply a product of its mode of existence or enterprise.[62]

> We must make up our minds to search for the secret of the national State in its specific inspiration as a State, in the policy peculiar to itself, and not in extraneous principles, biological or geographic in character. [P. 169]
> Renan discovered the magic word, filled with light, which allows us to examine, as by cathode rays, the innermost vitals of a nation, composed of these two ingredients: first, a plan of common life with an enterprise in common; secondly, the adhesion of men to that attractive enterprise. [P. 175]

Thus, as in the life of the individual, existence, purpose, and commitment become the core element in the life of the state. All else is simply a consequence of its common purpose and plan. The physical and natural characteristics of the state, as those of the individual, are instruments to justify policy rather than its cause.

A fundamental paradox that characterizes the very mode of existence of the modern state is that

> Uniformity as a means, is to change miraculously into multiplicity as an end; compulsion into freedom.[63]

This comment was intended as a basic criticism of Marxist doctrine; specifically, of its aspects advocating revolutionary overthrow of the capitalist regime to be followed by seizure of power and authority by a uniformly centralized proletarian dictatorship. This new state dictatorship has proved to be neither temporary nor has it totally succeeded in fostering a climate of "multiplicity" and "freedom" in which the pursuit of justice, equality, and democracy is able to endure. If in fact such revolution has brought change and perhaps marked improvement in the lot of the Marxist countries, it has certainly not led to the withering of the state as had been anticipated. The state as yet continues to be characterized by power, uniformity, and centralization that remains as a perennial obstacle to the attainment of "multiciplicity" and "freedom" for its people.

In a similar vein, Huxley,[64] in his monumental novel, *Brave New World,* alludes to the paradoxes that beset the policies of the supposedly more benevolent, enlightened Western nations. These contradictions revolve about the persistent and perennial human quest for freedom and choice in the face of the temptation to engineer and promote happiness, comfort, and convenience through the acceptance of uniformity and regularity as a way of life.

More specifically, in our country, varying degrees of inconsistency are clearly manifest in our policies of national conduct. As an example, the drastic means necessary to implement a version of democracy and freedom in a foreign country may very well lead to its undoing at home, as is indicated by concern in regard to problems of dissent dealing with the Viet Nam situation. This predicament issues from the situation in which the tenets of traditional Western democracy based on a government from "below" too often clash with the needs of both hot- and cold-war realities. These latter require a vast military, industrial, and political complex that rests on a heavily centralized, rigidly organized bureaucracy managed from "above." The crucial point of note is that under a variety of pretexts the collectivistic state in collaboration with the rampant individualism of industrial complexes seeks to promote a mode of existence consistent with its egoistic interest but at odds with its professed tradition, ideals, and heritage.

In so doing we witness the abdication of our commitment to the universal values of freedom and unity and at the same time man becomes ensnared in the following dilemma that characterizes our age:

> For a century man has moved ever deeper into a crisis which has much in common with others that we know from earlier history, but has one essential peculiarity. This concerns man's relation to the new things and connexions which have arisen by his action or with his cooperation. I should like to call this peculiarity of the modern crisis man's lagging behind his works. Man is no longer able to master the world which he himself brought about; it is becoming stronger than he is . . . and he no longer knows the word which could subdue and render harmless the golem he has created. Our age has experienced this paralysis and failure of the human soul successively in three realms. The first was the realm of technique. Machines which were invented in order to serve man in their work, impressed him into their service. They were no longer, like tools, an extension of man's arm, but man became their extension, an adjunct on their periphery, doing their bidding. The second realm was the economic. Production immensely increased in order to supply the growing number of men with what they needed, did not reach a reasonable coordination; it is as though the business of the production and utilization of goods spread out beyond man's reach and withdrew itself from his command. The third realm was the political. In the first World War, and on both sides, man learned with ever greater horror how he was in the grip of incomprehensible powers, which seemed, indeed, to be connected with man's will but which threw off their bonds and again and again trampled on all human purposes, till finally they brought all, both on this

side and on the other, to destruction. Man faced the terrible fate that he was the father of demons whose master he could not become. And the question about the meaning of this simultaneous power and powerlessness flowed into the question about man's being, which now received a new and tremendously practical significance.[65]

Man cannot afford to "lag" behind his potential to be free and to choose, either on the social or individual plane. For when he does he loses step with the ever-changing creative character of life. He is plunged into a state of despair and anguish from which he seeks refuge in collective violence and triviality or the fantasied world of individual idiosyncratic neurosis and psychosis.

In yet another vein, the neurotic utilizes his symptoms to preoccupy himself with acceptance by the Other so that he may avoid the necessity of self-scrutiny and thereby abdicate the perplexities of responsible action. Is it not likely that the contemporary drama with its ever present cold- and hot-war realities serves as a convenient pretext by which the state justifies its pursuit of similar tactics? The nation thus creates its enemies—where none need exist—as a pretext with which to occupy itself sufficiently so that it may turn its gaze from the task of creating within its own frontiers a nation of free and responsible people. Such diversionary tactics are relatively simple in the case of the state; the very same tactics are more difficult on the individual plane; in both dimensions the price to be paid is exorbitant.

An enemy of the nation is thus created and stamped with the ill repute of one who is unalterably evil and aggressive. The premise upon which such allegations are based may be challenged only with the utmost difficulty. The so-called enemy is strange and distant; as such there is little convincing evidence that can be cited to justify a point of view contrary to that of the formulators of national policy. The reasons for this are obvious. It is far more difficult to distract a people from domestic or internal problems; evidence at home is readily available and subject to various and conflicting interpretations depending on the needs of the vested interest group involved. Domestic issues are more likely to engender conflict and dissent; they may demand the unwanted ordeal of far-reaching self-scrutiny that would threaten egoistic interests. Further, ours is a collectivistic society that professes adherence to a democratic ideology, yet is not willing to make the sacrifices and commitment that are necessary if a viable democracy is to be sustained.

The nation, as with the neurotic individual, becomes preoccupied with the Other so that it is better able to shirk the difficulties of its own commitment to freedom and responsibility. The nation, however, need not resort to the drastic disguises that often account for the bizarre aspect of the neurotic symptom and which is necessary to secure his retreat. The state, through the power and impact of its institutional traditions and mass media, is able to codify a reality consistent with its common enterprise. Nevertheless, the nation eventually becomes bogged down in powerlessness as it persists in turning its gaze outward in an effort to avoid commitments that are ultimately inescapable. Its outward gaze is sustained very convincingly by the pressures exerted in the interests of the industrial-military requirements of contemporary reality. As it blindly pursues its technological advances it unwittingly bursts asunder the traditional framework of a democratic heritage with nothing new to replace it.

Our collectivistic state remains enticed by its technological prowess and achievement essentially managed from "above" in order all the more effectively to ignore the necessity of continually forging a new mainspring for democracy and responsibility. Again, as we shall see with the individual neurotic, the collective appears to prefer the ensuing state of powerlessness, confusion, and meaninglessness to the complex perilous task of creating a government "of the people, by the people and for the people"—the hallmark of a democratic ideal. Its powerlessness is reflected in the facility with which it proclaims the virtues of the "free world" while simultaneously unwilling to pursue the painstakingly difficult intermediate steps necessary to achieve and secure such a world. Effort and commitment in this direction are inescapable inasmuch as the ensuing collective powerlessness and aimlessness are totally futile. For in fact without such effort there follows an unprecedented eruption of violence and destruction that has characterized the modern era. What now is the meaning of individual powerlessness as depicted most glaringly in the stance of the neurotic?

VI. NEUROTIC INFRASTRUCTURE

I have suggested thus far that the symptom or suprastructure of neurosis unequivocally narrows the scope of the neurotic's existence which now dovetails with aspects of contemporary reality. The neurotic, sheltered by his symptoms, comes to believe that he is able to retreat from the risks of freedom and responsibility. The symptom is not at all intended to conceal either underlying complexes or aberrant instincts, but rather it is to permit and justify the neurotic in his effort to sustain his particular mode of existence. It is the neurotic's plan of action that underlies all his feelings, thoughts, ideas, and so forth, and which in turn give support to this plan. It is his mode of existence that I shall refer to as the infrastructure of neurosis. It consists of the neurotic's disposition to act in the world and experience himself as if he were powerless.

SYNDROMES OF POWERLESSNESS

It is the situation of the psychotic that epitomizes the condition of man's powerlessness. This condition is most extreme in the catatonic who has withdrawn from all engagement to a state of immobility and muteness. Other psychotic forms manifest themselves in fantasies of grandeur as well as in preoccupation with voices or visions. A fictitious world is thereby established in place of the oppressive unlivable real world that has been a reminder of one's powerlessness. The creation of this fictitious world provides the psychotic with a semblance of pride and at the same time enables him to perpetuate his stance of powerlessness in the real world.

The paranoid's preoccupation with accusatory hallucinations and other controlling influences has been interpreted as a means of assuaging his both sensed and real lack of power to act in a decisive fashion.[66] It is his anguish in this regard that he attempts to conceal via his belief that external controlling forces are responsible for his inaction. The anguish of this condition of powerlessness may be further buffered in assuming the role of a "Christ" or "Napoleon" as the "prestige" of such a role does away with the necessity for action.

The marked precariousness and fragility of the situation of the psychotic compared to that of the hysteric can once again be readily understood in terms of their respective freedom and power to act. The world view, experience, and self-concept of the psychotic is devoid of belief in his power to act autonomously; he therefore seeks refuge in the conviction that his precarious situation is not a reflection of his person but rather due to the "things that are being done to him." It is this conviction that serves as a face-saving device with which he may mollify his state of powerlessness. The hysteric, by contrast, is more inclined to act and is more willing to take the risk of such action. He does not act quite as powerlessly as does the psychotic and consequently can rely on less outlandish face-saving devices. Nevertheless, his mode of action is not truly free or productive; it is accompanied and conditioned by the classical hysterical symptoms of pain, paralysis, convulsion, and so forth. The actions of the hysteric are thereby rendered ineffectual, abortive, and ambiguous. As such, the hysteric by means of qualifying tactics creates the necessary alibis and excuses by which he protects his sense of worth in the face of apprehension and anticipated failure of his actions in view of the demands of his human situation.

We now turn to a brief exploration of syndromes encountered somewhat less frequently but characterized by the ostensibly bizarre manifestations of classical sadism and masochism. How are we to translate this apparent resort to crude instinctual behavior of either a sexual or aggressive form into terms that reflect the human situation of choice, freedom, and power? It has been theorized[67] that the intention of the sadist is to maintain his self-esteem by seeking to render his interlocutor helpless and powerless through either physical or verbal assault prior to engaging in an encounter with him. The sadist, furthermore, by focusing purely on the body is able to shield himself from the power that resides in the person, self, and mystery of the masochist. The masochist, for his part, in pleasurably accepting this situation of utter submissiveness is able to justify and persist in his experience of powerlessness. The actions of each are thus designed to protect their own self-esteem by vindicating their respective states of powerlessness through sadomasochistic tactics.

The neurotic or psychotic has utilized his experience to allow himself to be convinced that he must at all times act as if he were powerless—powerless to be free: powerless to tolerate the risk of becoming engaged in autonomous action based on intelligent self-reflecting decisions with consequent responsibilities. As one who acts powerless, he remains a spectator to significant events and decisions of his life that unavoidably further compound his dilemma. The meaning of the symptom for the patient now becomes evident; it is precisely that which enables him to persist in his role of one who is powerless and yet maintain a semblance of pride. What are both the origins and consequences of such conduct?

NEUROSIS AND THE OEDIPAL SITUATION

As has been mentioned, a relevant reinterpretation of the Oedipus complex must necessarily focus on the power struggle between parent and child rather than that of the rivalry based on sexual instinct if it is to be in accord with the realities of the human situation. It is the threat of oppression within the Oedipus situation that clearly obliges the child to forfeit his potential for spontaneity and with it the possibility for autonomous action in order that he placate the parental figures upon whom his very survival depends.

The powerlessness of the neurotic is further perpetuated as the mainspring of his mode of action is forged out of the internalized rules and doctrines of his parents and their culture. The incorporation of such rules begun during childhood often continues to heavily influence conduct during adulthood. Psychoanalysts have in this vein spoken of the transference phenomena.

It signifies the transferring of the forceful bond that exists between the neurotic and his forbears on to the person of the
analyst. It is basically a maneuver or tactic by which the patient seeks to perpetuate his familiar mode of existence that
depends on a continuing attempt to divest himself of power
and place it in the hands of the "Other." In the face of narrowed meaning possibilities one may have little choice but to
persist in such ways. The intensity of the transference situation
may thus reflect sociohistorical possibilities rather than unalterable instinctual drives.

The tragedy of man is therefore that as a child he is coerced
and duped into accepting and maintaining the role of weakness
which often has the effect of bolstering the self-esteem and
righteousness of those with whom he is in close association.
The child may be prodded and maintained in a position of inferiority, weakness, and helplessness above and beyond the
necessities of nature; furthermore, he must derive his self-
esteem from the shame of that very condition. He therefore
learns to base his pride on allowing others to decide for him;
his self-value becomes a measure of his blind obsequiousness.
Unfortunately, man is a creature of habit. As such, only with
much perseverance and effort will it be possible for him to out-
live his past in spite of the availability of more desirable alternatives.

The outcome of the overall Oedipal situation is that man becomes ensnared in an oppressive condition that has been aptly
described in the following Sartrian phrases:[68]

> We have given primacy to the object which we are to others
> over the subject we are to ourselves. [P. 43]
>
> He is not a man, he is a creature of man, entirely occupied by
> men. They have produced him, manufactured him out of whole
> cloth. Not a breath of air has been allowed to enter his soul.
> [P. 57]

Sartre signals the hurdles that man faces in his attempt to be
the very foundation of his existence. The neurotic condition
epitomizes man who believes that it is only the Other who may
decide and choose in equanimity. The neurotic in effect is the

embodiment of one who has had his freedom stolen from him. He continues, however, to remain unaware of the meaning or the urgency with which he must act to recoup his powers.

TO LIVE IN RETREAT

To what circumstances does the unresolved Oedipal situation lead? With what conflicts does it inevitably culminate? The neurotic has been duped into believing that it is only the Other who may bestow upon him a sense of worth. It is only the Other who has the power to delegate to him rights and privileges. When he does act it is only on the basis of "if" rather than "in spite of." Thus, he will act "if" he secures approval and acclaim. In other terms, he is primarily interested in acclaim; his actions are only a means towards this end. This is in effect tantamount to an abdication of the effort, commitment, and risk that must be made in spite of the adversity which is always inherent in the human situation and which must be overcome if one is to become himself. Let us look further at the case of Mrs. H.:

Such adversity may be based on Mrs. H.'s belief that firmness on her part may not be consistent with the wishes of her husband; she would thereby run the risk of rebuff; the threat of loneliness may then be brought to bear against her. Yet it is a risk one must take— a risk of at least being prepared to be alone as a price for the right to decide and to choose. The other alternative has been made clear to her: it is the suffering she has undergone during the years of her life. The difficulty for Mrs. H. under such circumstances is compounded. Not only is there the threat of rebuff, she is also faced with the plight perhaps similar to that of a pianist now obliged to perform a recital yet who at the same time has omitted months and years of preparation. Along these lines Mrs. H. recollects that as the youngest of three sisters she was repeatedly told, "You're too young to do anything on your own."

It was in obeying this admonition that her ways became most familiar and secure to her, though at the price of finding herself trapped in her current untenable condition. Her recollection also illustrates the manner in which perception of her personal biography is, in its essence, rather than a fact of life, one of many strategies by which she sustains herself in a role of helplessness and powerlessness. Having thus been admonished, and more what is important, having believed and lived in this spirit; it is not surprising that a persistent complaint of Mrs. H. is that she both lacks direction in her life as well as that she finds it difficult to know what she wants to do and where she should go. To believe that one does not know what to do may again be construed as a strategy to avoid the risk of acting or deciding and thereby taking the risks involved.

Along these lines Mrs. H. would at times query as to whether or not she in fact loves her husband. She remains as yet unaware of the inconsistency between love and coercive strategies. The latter is a means to obtain power for one's self; the former an end by which it is bequeathed to another. The difficulties involved were she to take the risk of loving her husband are revealed by her associations in which she recounts an incident: The other day the family had gone to a restaurant and she found herself unable to properly swallow her steak dinner. She brought to mind the events of the preceding night in which she had confessed to her husband that she had done rather poorly at bingo. Her inability to swallow her food reflects her unwillingness to tolerate the criticism that may be directed at her "right" to be inept at bingo. She retreats from her food as she does from others. Her retreat is further revealed as she recounts her persistent dizziness while shopping; this in regard to her concerns as to whether or not people are looking and judging her every move. It is only in the presence of her husband that such concerns are minimized.

Mrs. H. is convinced that she must seek power and security to survive. Unwilling to achieve this through the risk of self reliance, she unwittingly creates a sense of fragility and weakness about her person as a means of coercing the Other to give her power rather than to strive for a position of strength in which she may graciously bestow power upon others.

As is evident, all actions and conduct of the neurotic are conditioned wholly by the presence and power of the Other. He strives to seek recognition before rather than after his actions. He does not believe that he may "be" or "act" or "decide" on his own behalf; he is forced to exaggerate his weakness as his only known means of both survival and acclaim. To the extent that he is burdened by the Other he cannot be himself. As he cannot envision the possibility of being himself the notion of freedom becomes meaningless. Yet in spite of his pretense, alleged weakness, and apparent deference to the Other, he cannot avoid interest in his being. The neurotic is reliant on the Other yet is unable to transfer[69] * to the Other the entirety of his existence. He is both harassed and perplexed as he must retreat and live at the same time in order that he salvage his being. His suffering is the means whereby he secures his retreat as well as a measure of his inability to secure his being.

I would submit that it is this very precarious position together with its ominous consequences that in fact remains unadmissable or unconscious. This paradoxical condition must remain unknown or unconscious as long as more fruitful alternate modes of existence remain distant, unfamiliar, and unlikely possibilities upon which the patient may embark. Symptoms plague the patient only the better to accommodate him to the harsh realities of his condition as he experiences it. It will no longer be necessary for the neurotic to be plagued by his symptoms—to relinguish his freedom—if and when he is able to live and experience the meaning of the following words:

> And yet by not venturing it is so dreadfully easy to lose that which it would be difficult to lose in even the most venturesome venture, and in any case never so easily so completely as if it were nothing—oneself.[70]

A vicious circle ensues; man, who has become trapped by his experience of powerlessness, now finds it necessary to transcend this condition. However, too often to lose himself within the sphere of the collective is often as inimical to his being as are his neurotic choices. Thus the paradox and crisis heighten as what appear to be available alternatives within the social order are in actuality simply pseudo choices and thus to venture once again becomes too awesome to consider.

* The notion that life in fact is not transferable is rightfully emphasized in his works. Sartre states . . . "life is untransferable and that each man has to live his own; that no one can take over his task of living for him. . . ." There we have as concise a statement as any that points to the insoluble dilemma brought on by the attempt to forfeit one's individuality.

ALIENATION

Man's precarious paradoxical experience of powerlessness—his rejection of freedom—is always to some extent stamped into him by the pressure of social forces and trends. If this be the case, the phenomenon of mental illness as such has relevance for all contemporary life and is not solely a concern for the discipline of psychiatry. In fact it can be conceptualized as part of the overall problem of alienation already a main focus of study within the social sciences. Although often abused and by now commonplace, the concept of an alienation[71] is nevertheless crucial in the attempt to correlate individual powerlessness as exemplified by the phenomenon of mental illness with the social situation in which it is manifest. Alienation is the traditionally pivotal concept that has been employed by social scientists in their effort to implicate the realities of the social setting with the condition of individual powerlessness and malaise. If history is to be viewed as a narrative of a people's alienation, then an authentic social psychiatry must similarly recount the meaning of our patient's fall into this state of alienation in its entirety. What do I mean in suggesting that mental illness is a form of alienation?

Simply that it is the alienated individual who is powerless; it is he who is divested of his autonomy and individuality. The alienated man no longer considers himself as the source of power. In the same way the patient who is haunted by voices, overwhelmed by feelings of guilt, or obsessed by ruminations signals to us that he is trapped, and thus powerless to act in any positive sense. The person referred to as mentally ill therefore is preeminently the alienated individual. Or, in other terms, the concepts of alienation and mental illness do not refer to different kinds of people but rather to the different ways in which malaise and powerlessness may be manifested. Together mental illness and alienation signal the extent to which historical forces may undermine man as well as point to the necessity for social reconstruction in order that these forces be combated.

HUMAN CONDUCT:

MEDICINE OR MORALITY

-- *Chapter 7*

FROM BIOLOGY TO MORALS

I have attempted in the preceding chapter to suggest that neurotic patterns of living—as are all individual life styles—are woven out of the strands of the contemporary sociohistorical setting in its entirety. It remains now to pursue this effort by presenting further theoretical postulates with which to confront the long-standing anachronism that has served to obstruct the effort of correlating personal malaise with the structure of the social order in which it exists. This anachronism revolves about the fact that when such malaise is translated into terms of "illness" it is thereupon defined in terms of mechanistic happenings that depend on the interaction of nonhuman forces both within and outside man. These happenings are characterized by the absense of purpose, meaning, and volition and may now be considered as merely accidental to the human situation. As such they may be classified within the natural order that considers man to be a biological creature and thereby divorced from the realities of existence.

Although traditionally medicine is basically concerned with such happenings readily classified within the natural order and thereby supposedly divorced from the artifacts of history, one is struck by the words of the poet and physician Oliver Wendell Holmes:

> The truth is that medicine, professedly founded on observation, is as sensitive to outside influence, political, religious, philosophical, imaginative, as is the barometer to the changes of atmospheric density. Theoretically it ought to go on its own straightforward inductive path, without regard to changes of government or to fluctuations of public opinion. But [actually there is] a closer relation between the Medical Sciences and the conditions of Society and the general thought of the time, than would be first suspected.[72]

This apparently intimate relation of medicine to the conditions of society, nevertheless, remains indirect and accidental. Let me explain: The prevalence and severity of tuberculosis or diabetes within the populace bears of course on their socioeconomic status as well as the medical technology of the era. The presence of the disease, however, depends solely on the presence or absence of the tuberculosis bacillus or insulin hormone. In the instance of physical illness (happenings), the lines that separate the natural from the human order remain visible and well demarcated. Thus, in spite of the interaction of these two orders that may persist, the relationship nevertheless remains a peripheral one. By contrast, personal malaise as exemplified by mental illness is as centrally related to the social order as church-going is to Christianity.

In order to fully establish that the phenomenon which we refer to as mental illness is centrally related to events of the human order in much the same way as is the language we speak, it will be necessary to recast such phenomena from a biological-medical into a socio-political, ethico-moral (humanistic) framework. With this orientation we shall hope to be provided with the knowledge necessary to understand mental illness in so far as it signals the presence of inimical social forces which tend to aggravate the human plight writ large. Basically, we must be concerned with the forces of alienation and oppression that serve to transform man from a person into a thing. One manifestation of this transformation is the phenomenon we refer to as mental illness.

The purpose of this chapter then is to further bring to mind the significant correlation between the phenomenon of mental illness and the social order. It is also to provide a theoretical foundation by which the mechanistic model of mental illness may be converted into a humanistic one more suitable to a correlation with the totality of man's life situation. As such, the prevalence of mental illness—herein defined as the failure of man to fully negotiate his potential to be free—is to be taken as a signal of crisis within the social order. Individual suffering and malaise—one manifestation of which is mental illness—points to a crisis of meaning that in turn points to problems of choice and of freedom and at the same time to the existence of oppressing power and violence rather than to simple physical derangements. The former concepts fall wholly within the human order; the latter are explainable as happenings within the natural order.

Of primary importance, therefore, in establishing correlates between the phenomena of mental illness and the human situation in which it occurs is the need to reclassify such phenomena from the *natural* order to that of the *human or cultural* order. Implicit in this reclassification is the attempt to develop a humanistic theory of conduct based on purposes, meanings and situations rather than one reducible to physical dimensions. Amongst contemporary psychiatrists the works of Szasz, Laing, and Wheelis[73] imply, I believe, the necessity for just such a reclassification. In essence, they postulate that medical illness refers to deviations from normal anatomical-physiological structures and processes, whereas mental illness refers to human actions or conduct that is merely conventionally considered to be deviant from acceptable socioethical beliefs and conduct. Further, they suggest that such conduct is to be construed as purposeful and rational when interpreted within its social context rather than haphazard, chance happenings that reflect physical derangements. In other terms, medical illness refers to what one has; mental illness refers to what one is. The contention would seem to be borne out by classical anthropological and cross-cultural studies that depict the myriad ways of life, beliefs, and conduct of humans throughout the world; nevertheless, each pattern of life has meaning within its particular cultural context and cannot be reduced to any specific physical characteristics.[74]

If we are to assume that physical dimensions are incidental to the phenomenon of mental illness then it is no longer necessary to consider the mind as comparable to the body. For in fact the mind does not possess the physical characteristics of bodies occupying space and having weight; it therefore cannot be diseased in the manner of bodily organs. To make comparisons between the mind and body is therefore

> . . . a category-mistake. It represents the facts of mental life as if they belonged to one logical type or category . . . when they actually belong to another.[75]

As to the actual concept of mind:

> The styles and procedures of people's activities *are* the way their minds work and are not merely imperfect reflections of the postulated secret processes which were supposed to be the workings of minds. . . .[76]

In this vein with regard to the investigation of human conduct in general, it must be understood that

> Our inquiry is not into causes . . . but into capacities, skills, habits, liabilities and bents.[77]

The notion that the mind is comparable to an organ that houses unconscious impulses or emotions is one that must be questioned rather than simply taken for granted. Further, the mind as it is not a physical entity cannot be readily invoked in causal explanations of human conduct. To the contrary, man's mind if anything can be said simply to mirror man's conduct and action possibilities.

Parenthetically, it may be well to add that it was with the advent of Galenic medicine that a causal approach to human conduct came into fashion. All seemingly irrational behavior was thereupon construed as an outcome of internal pathology. Those who engaged in conduct that did not meet the requirements of conventional rules and prescriptions were considered "as if" sick. However, gradually the metaphorical qualifier "as if" was dropped and the metaphor was thereby converted to a myth[78] wherein human conduct came to be explained in physicalistic terms. I shall shortly explore the origins, significance, and ramifications of our human situation in which it becomes apparent that the metaphor-to-myth transition is basically a reflection of the mood and tenor of a mechanistic era that unwittingly seeks to understand man in terms of a machine. First, however, I wish to digress to comment upon a specific symptom—pain. When considered as an accidental happening it would be consistent to explain pain in terms of physical causality. By contrast, I wish to indicate how, in fact, pain may be approached from a fully humanistic, nonphysicalistic position consistent with its meaning as inherent rather than accidental to the patient's way of life. To do so it will be necessary to emphasize the dimension of freedom, choice, and responsibility. This interpretation of pain will exemplify the means whereby all psychiatric symptoms may be considered within these humanistic parameters. Not surprisingly, if we are to translate pain from the language of medicine to one of morals it will be necessary to restore the metaphorical qualifier "as if" and view pain as a purposeful subjective creation rather than a mechanistic isolated happening.

PAIN AS FICTION

Pain as an example of human tactics, strategy, and action rather than a physiological happening may be understood and comprehended wholly outside the dimension of physical causality. Only by means of a thoroughly humanistic approach to conduct in which we assume that man is viewed as one who acts "as if" he were a politician, student, in pain, and so forth, can we emphasize the importance of choice and purpose in conduct. I shall refer to this approach as a fictional conceptualization of pain and proceed to compare it with the traditional medical approach as well as the para-medical view often incorporated into the body of contemporary psychiatric theory.

I shall suggest at the outset that if we are to be concerned with matters of choice, awareness, and responsibility we may do well to conceptualize complaints of pain as a type of fiction. The concept of fiction once again implies that man's thoughts or actions cannot be substantiated or reduced to physical dimensions.[79] Instead we have to do with purpose, meaning, and consequences of our actions. Similarly the concepts of "freedom" and "responsibility" are themselves fictional in that they cannot be verified by recourse to physical parameters; it is rather a question of their meaning within the human situation.

The concept of pain as a fiction provides us with a most suitable springboard for an inquiry into the reasons for its choice, as well as its purpose and meaning. Implicit in a fictional view of pain is that it be comprehended apart from physical causation; this would logically facilitate inquiry into issues of choice and responsibility and therein lies its importance and usefulness. By contrast, the medical model of pain presupposes anatomical-physiologic derangements. Such derangements are involuntary "happenings," as are digestive or secretory functions and therefore do not entail the notion of responsibility or meaning.

Fictional pain, though not involved with physical sensation as we shall see below, nevertheless is a valid expression of the patient's life situation. Rather than a disorder, fictional pain may be considered to be a mode of conduct with ends and means that are not understood (unconscious) by the patient. Pain based on physical derangements, that we shall henceforth refer to as "medical" * pain, is, by contrast, accidental to the human situation. It is in this respect a meaningless happening —it simply "is"—as such it is irrelevant to a humanistic psychiatry that presupposes analysis of purpose and meaning.

* I wish to emphasize here that I shall not be concerned with pain arising from known pathological conditions such as ulcerative colitis, duodenal ulcer, etc. Pain in these instances has an obvious anatomical basis and therefore cannot be considered to be fictional.

A. FICTIONAL VERSUS MEDICAL PAIN

1. *Sensation*

The "primary" or medical model of pain may be explained simply on the basis of mechanical, physiochemical, or anatomical derangements that through increased physical stimulation of "nerve endings" cause pain.[80] The traditional psychologic or psychogenic model of pain simply substitutes in place of anatomical derangements aggressive or sexual impulses as the cause of pain.[81] Therefore to all intents and purposes it remains a mere facsimile of the medical model. A fictional view of pain, however, need not focus on physical or paraphysical happenings such as sensations or impulses. To the contrary, the notion of fictional pain obliges the therapist to be concerned solely with the purposes, methods, and motives of the patient's conduct.

The divergence of these two approaches to pain is brought out vividly in the following remarks:

> . . . we cannot characterize visual or auditory sensations as we can listening or observing as being careful or careless, cursory or sustained, methodical or haphazard. . . . We observe from inquisitiveness or obedience but we do not have tickles from this or any other motive. . . .[82]

And further,

> . . . [one] may show skill, patience and method in peering, but not in having visual sensations.[83]

From this we may conclude that it is appropriate to compare the concept of fictional pain with that of such concepts as listening, observing, and peering—conduct or action that involves motives, skills, and purposes. Whereas, by contrast, medical pain is comparable to visual or auditory sensations that are explained only on the basis of physical happenings. Yet another comparison may be the difference that exists between a corpse and one who plays the role of a corpse. The former, as with medical pain, is explainable on the basis of physiochemical happenings while the latter as with fictional pain is a matter of motives, purposes, and skills. Inasmuch as we have suggested that fictional pain cannot be reduced to physical sensations, how may we interpret its existence?

2. Cause or Consequence

The traditional model of medical pain is linked to the concept of causality. This cause-effect model of pain is mechanistic and operates beyond the awareness or control of the patient. I shall attempt now to demonstrate that the fictional-humanistic view of pain by contrast is concerned not with "causes" but rather with "consequences" that cannot be considered apart from patient, choice, and responsibility. The view of pain as "fiction," thus far, entails the notion of purpose, skills, and methods. Any attempt to interpret such phenomena in terms of "causality" would be

> . . . improper in much the same way as is the question, What transactions go on between the House of Commons and the British Constitution? [84]

These comments would imply that medical and fictional dimensions of pain involve different categories of events. Only the former (medical) category can be explained on the basis of "causal happenings" while the latter cannot. In fact the latter (fictional) view must be understood without resort to the invoking of happenings. In the absence of happenings (sensation) it is not possible to invoke "causal" explanation as a basis for pain as is the case in the medical approach. How then do we account for such pain?

Fictional pain, as we have stated, may be viewed as a mode of conduct; the playing of a role that is based upon one's belief and conviction. Human beings as actors are easily convinced of the authenticity of the roles they play. One is what he does.

> One feels more ardent by kissing, more humble by kneeling and more angry by shaking one's fist. That is, the kiss not only ex-

presses ardor but manufactures it . . . the professor putting on an act that pretends to wisdom comes to feel wise. The preacher finds himself believing what he preaches.[85]

Similarly, fictional pain is not "caused" by physiological happenings but is "manufactured" through the act of effortless, unreflecting commitment to the role of one who is sick and in pain. Fictional pain is therefore both a creation and "consequence" of the sick role that the patient has chosen albeit for reasons of which he may not be aware.

3. Authenticity

I have argued that fictional pain is a phenomenon that need not be explained by resorting to the discovery of evidence for the presence of physical happenings, namely, sensation. What then may we say regarding the authenticity of such pain? Can the patient really experience pain in the absence of concrete physical causal factors? Does such pain exist in view of the fact that we do not have recourse to clinical or laboratory data upon which to verify or substantiate its presence?

The question of authenticity can perhaps best be understood by making several appropriate analogies from the field of religion. The significance of religious beliefs is often similarly challenged by the suggestion that such beliefs are unsound, unscientific, lack any tangible physical evidence upon which they can be verified, and so on. Thus, it has often been fashionable in theological circles to debate issues such as whether, for instance, Moses really existed. There were those who patronizingly concluded that it mattered little whether or not he did exist. The crucial issue was simply the significance and meaning of the life and deeds ascribed to Moses for his descendants of yesteryear and today. Or, in a similar vein, is it imperative to interpret biblical stories of the Creation or the Fall in terms of a specific time or place? Is it necessary that the drama enacted at Mount Sinai be reduced to its acoustic or optical dimensions in order that it retain its significance?

It becomes obvious that the reliance on physicalistic explanations is in these instances unnecessary. In fact, any attempt to reduce these events and narratives to physicalistic terms would be tantamount to depriving them of their monumental meaning and significance for civilization. Similarly we may then conclude from these analogies that the only relevant issue for the psychotherapist—in contrast to the task of the physician—is to explore the meaning and significance of pain, not to determine either its location or its veracity. This very quest for certainty and verifiability is advantageous in the domain of physical medicine. In so far as it concerns psychotherapy, the more one focuses on pain as having a "cause" within the body, the more difficult the task of analyzing its meaning and relevance to the total life situation of the patient (Chapter 9).

B. HYSTERIA AND MALINGERING

We have heretofore been occupied with the task of signaling essential differences in the conceptualization of the "medical" compared to the "fictional" approach to pain. I have affirmed that the latter approach is singularly conducive to confrontation and elucidation of the issues of volition and responsibility within the context of psychotherapy (Chapter 9). By way of contrasting the tactics of the hysteric with that of the malingerer I shall proceed with a further comparison of the medical and fictional methods of approach to pain.

1. Varieties of Make-Believe

The task of distinguishing between the hysteric and the malingerer is often a pseudoproblem that in practice would hardly seem necessary to pursue.* However, for our theoretical purposes, let us inquire further into this matter. In order to distinguish between a diamond and an imitation we must resort to

---

* It should be realized that the issue of malingering is mainly of relevance to the institutional psychiatrist who has within his power to take action either for or against the patient's behalf. As such it may become necessary for the "captive" patient to contrive in order that he achieve ends otherwise difficult to obtain.

physical techniques that allow us to establish differences in their respective physical characteristics. Resort to physical techniques, however, is not of value in attempting to distinguish between the hysteric and the malingerer, whose "traits" cannot be reduced to physical dimensions in spite of the fact that the former has traditionally been considered to be "genuinely sick" and the latter an imposter. Why not? Simply because *both* the hysteric and malingerer merely *resemble someone* having pain rather than *have something resembling pain.* In a similar vein, the effectiveness of the player in the parlor game of charades who picks the card "pain" depends on his skills and capacities in an effort to resemble someone having pain rather than on the actual experiencing of any anatomico-physiological sensation.

The performances of both hysteric and malingerer depend on their respective motives, purposes and goals. It is therefore not correct to imply that the hysteric is someone who experiences vague or faint sensations totally absent in the individual who is suspected of malingering. Neither the pain of the hysteric nor that of the malingerer is a happening; rather both create and utilize pain as a tactic or device to obtain particular ends.

Where then does the difference lie between the hysteric and malingerer? Ryle's eloquent statement provides us with some thoughts as to how this dilemma may be resolved:

> . . . in some varieties of *make believe* the pretender is deliberately simulating, in some varieties he may not be quite sure to what extent he is simulating and in other varieties he is completely taken in by his own acting. . . . The fact that people can fancy that they see things, are pursued by bears, or have a grumbling appendix without realizing that it is nothing but fancy is simply a part of the unsurprising general fact that not all people are all the time at all ages and in all conditions as judicious or critical as could be wished.[86]

It is obvious then that the malingerer possesses the critical insight and judiciousness that elude the hysteric; nevertheless, both individuals engage in varieties of "make believe" * not at all reducible to physical dimensions. It is of course the task of therapy to inquire into the realities of the human condition and the reasons that prompt the hysteric to adopt this unreflecting "make believe" pattern of conduct.

2. Deception

As complaints of pain on the part of the hysteric or malingerer cannot be verified through clinical or laboratory procedures we may arbitrarily suggest that their sufferings be considered types of deception. How does the deception of the hysteric differ from that of the malingerer?

It is simply that the hysteric deceives himself as well as others. He is "taken in" by his own deception and is not aware of his intention to deceive both others and himself. The intention of the malingerer is to deceive but he does not hide such intentions from himself. He is the deceiver while the other is the deceived. Not so with the hysteric who is both deceiver and deceived.[87] †

It is well to mention at the conclusion of this analysis that has dealt with pain in terms of fictions, make-believe and deceptions, that our intention here has not been to cast aspersions on the integrity of our patients. There is no indication that our patients are less honest than other individuals. We may only conclude that their fictions are less fruitful than those of others. Furthermore, has it not been said that the sincere man is he who is simply taken in by his own propaganda?

In conclusion, I have alluded to some of the inconsistencies that often beset the psychiatrist in his approach to pain. These consist in the conceptualization of pain in reference to "causes,"

---

* In using the term "make believe" it is well to point out that the fictional or flimsy nature of the complaint on one hand makes it necessary for the patient to persist as he does in his complaint; but on the other hand allows him the possibility of choosing an alternate mode of conduct once he is aware of his "make believe" pain.

† See the chapter on Bad Faith for the further philosophical implications in regard to the position of "deceiver and deceived" which are beyond the scope of this work.

"sensation," "repressed instinct," terms that obscure patient responsibility on one hand, while yet on the other, psychotherapy, as we shall see, is conducted on the assumption that the meaning and purpose of pain is created by the patient. I have intimated the possibility of a logical impasse that arises in the effort to reconcile divergent categories of events, i.e., "happenings" with "purposes," "sensation" with "meaning," etc. It is to this schism between the *mechanistic* and *humanistic* dimensions to which Sartre refers when he states that psychiatry has discovered the "lie without the liar." A fictional approach to pain would seem to resolve this schism in favor of illuminating the significance of the patient's choice to "be" in pain. It emphasizes his possibilities of choice rather than causes that lie beyond his active powers. Let me now proceed to a further exploration of this schism and attempt to relate it to the realities of our sociohistorical setting.

MAN: PERSON OR THING?

In the same way that human conduct in general and neurosis in particular is basically a sociohistorical artifact, so psychiatric theory itself is a product of our age and thus has been markedly influenced by the tenor of the times. Classical psychoanalytic practice is fundamentally a technique devised to enhance man's freedom and choices. Ironically, it has itself become bogged down in theoretical constructs heavily weighted with deterministic-causalistic baggage which obviously undermines its effort to signal to man that he need not continue to be what he is. There thus persists until today an intertwining of mechanistic and humanistic strands; let us examine the origin and ramifications of these two apparently conflicting strands that lie at the heart of psychoanalysis.

Historically, both European and American psychiatry have been characterized by long-standing controversy as to the merits of a somatic-naturalistic approach versus that of a psychological-moral approach to the problem of mental illness. The concept of insanity as an outgrowth of moral rather than physical aberrations was widely discussed as far back as the nineteenth century. The notion of moral insanity[88] as an outcome of emotional liability gradually led to the concepts of modern analytic psychology which is ostensibly at odds with the narrower somaticist approach. Nevertheless, in spite of the present-day popularity and influence exerted by the various schools of analytic psychology, the phenomenon of mental illness continues to come under the jurisdiction of the field of medicine presided over by the medical expert who tends to view such phenomena as *happenings* rather than creations.

Why is it that in spite of the efforts of the analytic schools to provide a humanistic framework that would allow for an interpretation of the phenomenon of mental illness in terms of meaning, motive, and purpose—concepts antithetical to a mechanistic-causal approach to mental illness—it is nevertheless the latter approach that continues to hold sway? In order that this dilemma be clarified one must keep in mind the dictum that

> Not what we call science determines life but our conception of life determines what should be acknowledged as science.[89]

This would, in short, imply that the contemporary predominence of the medical approach to mental illness rests not on the evidence of so-called pure scientific research and investigation but has become entrenched in accordance with the mood of our sociohistorical era. The ways of our life therefore create and mold science into a form consistent with the needs of our situation. One may therefore conclude that the persistent popularity of the medical mechanistic approach to mental illness is best understood when it is realized that this approach is fundamentally an outcome as well as a support to the mechanistic tenor and demands of our time. A method of inquiry and investigation into the significance of mental illness (deviant conduct) consistent with a humanistic framework would necessitate an interpretation of such phenomena in terms of their relevance to our socio-historical setting rather than one reducible to physicalistic explanation. This approach continues to be largely ignored as a result of what Mills has referred to as "methodological inhibition." [90] As such, the method of approach to a problem (mental illness) is thus determined not by its inherent requirements but rather by applying to it technological and physicalistic techniques that satisfy the demands of an era. Such inhibition leads to the inevitable transformation of man into a thing. It is consistent again with an age of technology that rests on a base of collectivism, impersonalization, and functionalization—on man's alienation from himself.

HISTORICAL INTERLUDE

Foucault, in a little-known but nevertheless masterly historical work, indicates that the quest to confront and grasp the meaning of madness has ironically been hindered rather than furthered by the advent of the modern naturalist-physicalist approach that has placed its emphasis on simple treatment or custodial care. In this regard, he states:

> Classicism felt a shame in the presence of the inhuman that the Renaissance has never experienced [91]

and continues

> . . . madness had become a thing to look at: no longer a monster inside oneself but an animal with a strange mechanism.[92]

The introduction of the concept of madness as a "mechanism" was part of the process of medicalizing madness; it eventually became synonomous with the loss of dialogue between madness and reason. This dialogue, Foucault ironically implies, lingered to the beginnings of the modern era in the form of the physical struggle over internment that often ensued between patient and asylum keeper. This would perhaps suggest that rather than fostering dialogue between "madness" and reason the humaneness and kindness that later characterized midnineteenth-century psychiatry was at least in part a charitable paternalistic gesture offered to those considered inferior and unworthy of serious contention. In the twentieth century the dialogue came to a halt as madness came to be considered an illness as diabetes; confinement, hospitalization, and treatment under the guise of humaneness came to be the order of the day, thereby obviating the necessity for fruitful dialogue between madness and reason.

THE DILEMMA OF PSYCHOANALYSIS: HAPPENING OR MEANING?

The pervasive influence of the sociohistorical setting in which psychoanalysis has emerged has given rise to a fundamental paradox that lies within the body of its theories. This dilemma is heightened as we attempt to establish a degree of consistency within a theory of psychoanalysis that interprets symptoms in terms of both meaning and causes at one and the same time. How is man to be considered a *person* and a *thing* simultaneously? How is *humanism* to be reconciled with *mechanism*? Meaning, it must be understood, depends on the purposes and motives of conduct engaged in by the spontaneous, subjective individual. By contrast, causes refer to facts that just "are" and therefore entail the postulation of neither meaning nor responsibility. This fundamental dichotomy has been expressed as follows:

> On the one hand in clinical practice, and especially through the technique of free association, it [psychoanalysis] assumes a spontaneous subject; on the other it reifies the concept of mind and elaborates a scientific type theory in terms of causes.[93]

This schism becomes more apparent as we shall further contrast the theory and practice of psychoanalysis (Chapter 9). The former is essentially devoted to a mechanistic-naturalistic explanation; the latter to a psychological interpretation of meaning and purpose.

RAMIFICATIONS OF PSYCHOANALYTIC THEORY

In this regard Freud has written:

> It is the therapeutic technique alone that is purely psychological; the theory does not by any means fail to point out that neuroses have an organic basis—though it is true that it does not look for that basis in any pathological-anatomical changes, and provisionally substitutes the conception of organic functions for the chemical changes which we should expect to find but which we are at present unable to apprehend.[94]

The implication is clear; psychoanalytic theory views the psyche as a reflection of the vicissitudes of biological instincts. In the same way that a camera lens refracts and projects light, the mind automatically reflects instinctual and libidinal drives. In other terms, psychoanalytic theory ascribes to the mind the mechanism, automaticity, and regularity that have otherwise characterized Newton's "billiard ball" universe. The mind has therefore been construed as analogous to the physical body.

The total structure of man is thereby objectified and reduced to nothing but libido and aggression. Libidinal and aggressive instincts are equated with the entirety of man's structure rather than inserted into its totality. The part is taken for the whole. Libido and aggression are considered to explain phenomena rather than to be explained.

Instinctual drives within psychoanalytic theory are construed as abstract happenings that do not bear any relevance to concrete social circumstances. Man is viewed as a product of nature. The self is negated as a precipitate of the social order as all social phenomena are considered simply as secondary, irrelevant, or rationalization of man's instinctual drives.

The language of instincts is suggestive of a basic polarization between the individual and society. It intimates that the former harbors within himself antisocial urges that lie beyond his power or reason; at one and the same time he is a suspect of evil-doing yet declared irresponsible. Man is viewed as inevitably conflict-ridden by virtue of his instinctual endowment; he is at odds with himself. Oppressive social structures are invoked as necessary solely to tame man's instincts but are otherwise absolved from liability for the difficulties that beset man. Human conduct is thus viewed as automatic, abstracted from the realities of man's situation. Man is regarded as a mere happening. Such, I believe, are some of the unfortunate implications of psychoanalytic *theory*. The meaning of its immense contribution, however, to psychiatry, science and man will be lost or distorted unless we take care to elaborate upon the rich meaning of its *technique* and *practice*, and we shall shortly do so.

THE UNCONSCIOUS: MEANS OR END?

In order further to emphasize the contrast between purpose and cause, between humanism and mechanism, at this point it would be useful to focus exclusively on the concept of the unconscious; and more specifically to suggest the relation that exists between the classical psychoanalytic theory of the unconscious and what I have referred to as a mechanistic-naturalistic explanation of neurotic conduct. If one were to take the Freudian psychoanalytic framework literally, the unconscious would be tantamount to a niche or recess into which are repressed the various traumatic emotions, affects, impulses, and instincts. In his well-known metaphor of the "iceberg" Freud suggests that it is from this hidden recess that affect and impulses exert their ominous causal role in human conduct. The patient is thereby conceptualized as a hapless victim of complex "unconscious instinctual" forces operating beyond both his grasp and his understanding. Man becomes a passive host whose psyche serves as a battleground for the conflicting forces of the id and super ego. An unfortunate impression likely to be conveyed is that the outcome of this conflict is beyond the influence of the individual and as such he is basically powerless to determine his proper mode of conduct.

It is instincts, then, that lie at the core of psychoanalytic theory of the unconscious:

> We thus find our first conception of the essential nature of an instinct by considering its many characteristics, its origin in sources of stimulating within the organism and its appearance as a constant force, and thence we deduce one of its further distinguishing features; namely, *that no actions* of flight avail against it.[95]

Therefore the interpretation of symptoms or conduct in terms of meaning and purpose presented by the responsible spontaneous subject is clearly minimized in favor of explanations based on unconscious internal instinctual derivatives reducible to unalterable physical dimensions. Phenomena delegated as natural and unalterable presuppose neither meaning nor purpose. The unconscious in this vein becomes a fixed end; what man does is portrayed as both involuntary and inevitable.

In contrast to the mechanical Freudian concept of the unconscious with its naturalistic overtones that is literally construed as an end or region into which instincts and affects are repressed and within which conflicts are generated, a humanistic conceptualization requires a man-centered theory of the unconscious based exclusively on purpose and meaning. The latter concept of the unconscious is in accord with a belief in man's potential to strive toward as well as create goals and ends for himself rather than be driven solely by mechanistic causes. It is this notion that is implied by the following:

> What might otherwise be regarded as the termination; namely, the specific disease, now takes its proper place as a means, a method of life, a symptom indicative of the past taken by the patient to attain his goal of superiority.[96]

Similarly, a humanistic theory of the unconscious does away with the necessity for it to serve as a basis for explanation in terms of mechanistic-antecedent causality but rather as an investigative tool with which to scrutinize the motives, purposes, and meaning of an individual's way of life. The unconscious is therefore not a "region" into which affects are repressed; rather it is simply a matter of what is unknown or "not understood." Actions that are conveniently "not understood" become all the more useful as purposeful tactics or means (as any other symptom) utilized in the quest of particular ends as mentioned in the previous chapter.

THE PRACTICE AND TECHNIQUE OF PSYCHOANALYSIS

In contrast to the theory of psychoanalysis, its technique is indicative of a marked concern for the spontaneity, subjectivity, and uniqueness of the individual. Psychoanalysis after all originated as a method of liberating the patient whose freedom to act has been compromised. Psychiatric symptoms, as I have suggested, are in fact the means by which man driven by adversities in his life situation attempts to portray himself as if he were neither free nor responsible. In short, he acts as if he were a victim of causes. Freud's intuitive and implicit awareness of this very meaning of neurotic symptoms markedly influenced the form and technique that would later characterize psychoanalytic practice. It is this, perhaps, more than anything else that spells out the genius of the man. However, the overwhelming desire to win support and firmly establish the young science of psychoanalysis made it necessary that he accommodate its theoretical framework to that of the prestigious natural sciences. These currents led to the basic and fundamental logical impasse which has ever since plagued psychoanalysis and with it contemporary psychiatry.

It is in considering the practice of psychoanalysis rather than its theory that we may more readily understand the reasons for which Freud, early in his career, astutely refrained from the use of techniques laden with authoritarian overtones such as hypnosis, physical examinations, involuntary therapy, and so forth. It became apparent to him that these techniques would only have furthered the patient's inclinations to remain a distant, passive spectator. To have persisted in such techniques would have been for the therapist to encourage the patient's continued indulgence in the conviction that he was both help-less and irresponsible and thereby lend support to the very im-pression that neurotic symptoms seek to establish and confirm. Other techniques and problems encountered in the practice of psychoanalysis such as problems of counter transference and termination of therapy may be viewed in a similar perspective (Chapter 9). Freud was obviously determined that psychoa-nalysis develop into a technique that would maintain the high-est regard for both patient accountability and spontaneity. The aim, therefore, of psychoanalytic practice is to facilitate action based on freedom and choice rather than to further the process of self-intimidation and subjugation for which the patient un-wittingly creates his symptom. The meaning of the symptom as man's effort to curtail his freedom must be explored further.

THE SYMPTOM: INTENTIONAL OR ACCIDENTAL?

The impasse within psychoanalysis, as already alluded to, is characterized by the mechanism and determinism of psychoa-nalytic theory on one hand and on the other the humanistic inclination to view man as a purposeful spontaneous subject. It as yet remains unresolved. This impasse will only be resolved when in both theory and practice man is consistently viewed as wholly responsible and free. It is for this reason that the symp-tom ought be regarded as a *consequence of purpose* rather than a *product of cause;* as reflecting man's awareness of his future rather than a simple atavism.

In this regard let me explore the possibilities and ramifica-tions of conceptualizing symptoms wholly in terms of purposes and tactics. If this be the case, I must be concerned primarily with the uses and consequences to which depression, hostility, and anxiety are put rather than attempting to explain them in terms of causality. The traditional medical investigation of a symptom such as anxiety, it must be recalled, points toward an etiological factor such as organ dysfunction as in the case of thyroid disease. The psychotherapist who is determined to il-luminate the dimensions of man's freedom must resist the temptation to compete with his medical colleague by engaging in paramedical investigations of anxiety as a product of man's physical endowment, thereby nullifying the dimensions of his freedom. The search within man—the emphasis on intrapsychic conflict—unavoidably neglects the oppressive realities of man's existence. A paramedical reductionistic orientation in regard to the psychiatric symptom provides easy refuge from the arduous and challenging task of correlating the symptom with the entire meaning of life that must obviously transcend the limitations of man's bodily mechanisms.

An explanation of violence, for instance, reducible to instinctual derivatives is tantamount to exonerating the revolting conditions of man's social circumstance as well as obfuscating the insecurities of life itself in favor of stressing facile biological explanations. The latter explanation fails to come to grips with the possibility of violence and anger as man's response to his life circumstance.

Our insistence on interpreting the psychiatric symptom as meaningful is part of the overall effort of portraying man as one who is both free and responsible. Man who is free is unavoidably concerned with his future; his past becomes a purposeful creation in order that he be more satisfactorily sustained in his future conduct. The psychoanalytic preoccupation with causes as well as man's unalterable past reflects pessimism in regard to the necessity and possibility for man to be free and to make new choices. The psychoanalytic focus on the past is linked to its view of the symptom as a product of causes. When man is construed as a causal happening of his past, present-day reality having much to do with the purpose and meaning of the symptom may too often be given short shrift.

The following supposition in regard to psychoanalytic procedure by an astute critic of the field is, I believe, illustrative of this point:

> When he [the patient] dwells on some topic or when he displays great emotion the analyst will tend to suggest an interpretation to him of what he is saying. The more the analysis progresses the more the patient will pass from talk about adult

life to talk about childhood and incidences that have apparently been forgotten will be recalled. This recalling will be accompanied by an emotional release. Such emotional release will in turn be followed by mitigation of the neurotic's symptoms which were the occasion of undertaking psychoanalytic treatment.[97]

This rather common interpretation of psychoanalytic procedure emphasizes its view of the symptom as an outcome of past-causality. It therefore has the effect of minimizing the significance of present-day social circumstances; furthermore, this deterministic outlook implies that inquiry into these circumstances is of little importance. It is therefore only when the symptom is considered as a reflection of the predicament of a free purposeful individual that consideration will be given to the full circumstances of his life. Is it not possible that man's conduct in fact reflects an attachment to his past—not causally determined—but as a purposeful evasion of what he considers to be the real or created oppressiveness of his life circumstance? If we are seriously to consider individuals as responsible the symptom must be interpreted in terms of its use—principally in self-esteem maintenance. At issue is not an atavistic remnant but the meaning of the neurotic's life situation in its entirety.

FROM WITHIN TO WITHOUT

Thus in contrast to the interpretation of the symptom as a product of causes we prefer the conceptualization of the symptom as purposeful in that it may well signal to us the importance of social crisis as a significant dimension of individual malaise. The phenomenon of mental illness in this light is taken to indicate social crisis; a failure on the part of the social order to provide adequate possibility for its members to lead a satisfying existence.

Mental illness, as we know it, is above all else an unwillingness, inability, or reluctance on the part of the patient to fully participate in the ongoing events of the day. The patient retreats to a private world with his own tasks and concerns as a means of sustaining his self-esteem. The phenomenon of mental illness may thus be construed in one of its dimensions as a form of *social protest—ineffective as it may be.* The medicalization of this phenomenon, however, has discredited it as a form of protest by reducing its significance to one of physical dimensions or intrapsychic conflict that originates wholly within the individual himself. The symptom when construed as purposeful rather than accidental allows psychiatry the possibility of reversing this trend. It then becomes feasible and in fact necessary that psychiatry align itself within the momentous tradition of the Enlightenment, dedicated to the development of reason and criticism that points beyond the bounds of the individual to the social origins of evil.

A revitalized post-Freudian psychology must emphasize not man's accommodation to society but rather allow man to maximize his possibilities and thereby confront the restrictive forces of the social order. A post-Freudian psychology must transcend the notion that man is basically against himself, unalterably plagued by intrapsychic conflict abstracted and divorced from the social realities of the day. Psychiatry must confront and comprehend the total experience from which neurosis and psychosis is derived rather than simply explain it away.

The phenomenon of mental illness does not simply reflect unruly forces within man (Chapter 8) but rather those that exist within the fabric of society as well. It is these forces at the level of the family, community, and society at large that must be scrutinized and which must become the very subject of psychiatric investigation if the effort to link the meaning of personal misery with the social issues from which they are derived is to persevere.

An authentic post-Freudian psychology must align itself with elements of the pre-Freudian psychiatry concerned with man within the world rather than exclusively with what is within man. This concern is exemplified in the following remarks by Maudsley, a nineteenth-century English psychiatrist:

> Multiplied industries and eager competition can scarcely fail to augment the liability to mental disease. The occupation which a

man is entirely engaged in does not fail to modify his character and the reaction upon the individual nature of a life which is being spent with a sole aim of becoming rich is most vainful. The exclusiveness of this life aim and occupation too often saps the moral law or altruistic element in his nature and in his person deteriorates the nature of humanity.[98]

If we are to achieve a meaningful social psychology it must develop in the spirit of the following words explaining a phenomenon such as feelings of inferiority:

> If there is an inferiority complex, it is the outcome of a double process:—primarily, economic;—subsequently the internalization of this inferiority.[99]

It suggests that human conduct—individual or group—reflects the realities of economic and social conditions. Desires and wishes are not to be explained psychologically but rather socially. An inferiority complex refers not to accidental or organic deficiencies but rather to the internalization of oppressive conditions which promote feelings of inferiority that has similar meaning and origins, whether they exist in the family of the neurotic or the colonial situation of the black man. In broader terms Fanon suggests that the impulsivity and instinctual-like violence of the Algerian does not reflect disorder within the central nervous system but rather is an answer to the revolting conditions of colonial oppression. In fact, the circumstances of neurosis may be considered as a microcosmic facsimile of an oppressive colonial situation.*

A science of psychiatry that pursues investigation of nervous disorder distracts and diverts attention from oppressive social conditions. It in fact not only condones these conditions but in doing so compounds the problem of neurosis which has its

---

* In other terms, I believe that there are many parallels between the life style of the neurotic and other oppressed peoples—Blacks, Jews, colonized and so forth. Each of these groups experiences oppression and each must free himself in his own way. In an as yet unpublished manuscript "Perspectives in Oppression: the Patient and Psychiatrist," I have analyzed in detail the meaning of oppression insofar as the neurotic and other oppressed groups are concerned.

origin in these very sources. Any attempt to reduce the problem of the neurotic condition to terms of naturalistic biology in effect serves to exacerbate this condition of powerlessness (the core element of neurosis), as the social order which perpetuates this condition is now no longer liable to scrutiny. Such attempts fail to comprehend violence, laziness, phobias, or compulsions—as the case may be—as a tactic by which man maintains his self-esteem in the face of overwhelming powerlessness. It is oppressive social conditions that promote such powerlessness and that will continue to remain unchecked if the search for the "intrapsychic" version of the "twisted conduct—twisted molecule" formula continues unabated.

EXISTENTIAL DIMENSION

 *Chapter 8*

THE SIN-NEUROTIC COMPLEX

I have thus far considered the "self" as a precipitate of the social dimension of existence. In so far as man is a moral animal he is one who may question the meaning of his actions. The meaning of his actions must be considered not only from the perspective of social parameters (social structures and institutions) but from the totality of existence itself. Further, the social dimension itself must be comprehended in terms of the totality of human existence, as I shall shortly indicate. I intend in this chapter to focus on the oppression inflicted on man and his institutions by the existential dimensions of existence; in other terms, we now have to do principally with Time rather than Space.

In conceptualizing neurosis as a moral problem I hope to have laid the groundwork that will allow us to comprehend and draw conclusions in terms of both the existential and social dimension of existence. The moral problem of freedom, choice, and responsibility is inseparable from the dimension of Time. It is principally in view of the problem of Time that it becomes necessary to act and choose. If we lived forever these crucial matters would be less relevant. Our concern with Time must not be explained away as a neurotic symptom itself; rather our discussions thus far as to the significance of human conduct in general and neurosis in particular must be anchored within the dimension of Time. It will be in confronting the dimension of Time and ultimately the meaning of life itself that we shall be able to interpret neurotic conduct rather than reduce the problem of life to a mere projection of neurotic tendencies.

I shall attempt to correlate the problems of neurosis with the oppression that Time and existence bring to bear against man by way of establishing a comparison with the age-old concept of sin. The concept of sin has traditionally been invoked when considering man's action within the totality of the meaning of human existence. As such I shall endeavor to draw parallels between the universal concept of sin and that of neurosis and refer to the similarities as the sin-neurotic complex. One implication of this term is that sin and neurosis do not refer to two entirely different kinds of conduct, but to different manifestations of essentially similar conduct that have much to do with each other. Another is that the concept of sin as well as that of neurosis can be said to describe conduct that is a reflection of fundamental anxieties. In other words, the anxieties of existence that urge man towards the state of sin are the very ones that prompt him to neurotic conduct. Neurosis in this regard becomes a particular stance or response—amongst others—to the demands of existence rather than simply a naturalistic phenomenon divorced from the totality of the human situation. I shall endeavor to demonstrate that in this regard neurosis is one language amongst many, one strategy amongst others, by which man copes with the problem of human existence. The neurotic, viewed from a humanistic framework, in his actions, as anyone else, communicates the saga of his life situation rather than simply reflecting internal accidental derangements. It therefore becomes necessary that we inquire into the fundamental aspects of the human condition that lie at the source of both sin and neurosis in order to establish a correlation between these two concepts. Put otherwise, it will be my task to suggest that sin and neurosis represent ill-fated attempts to resolve the problems of life.

THE NATURE OF SIN

The much debated issue of the origin of sin is beyond the scope of this work. My comments on the problem of sin will be descriptive rather than explanatory. I therefore shall not be concerned with whether sin is inherent in man's structure, whether it is simply inevitable in man's existence or still further, whether sin is a product of a particular historical situation.

The phrase "finite-freedom" has been utilized to characterize the tension between man's basic ontological character and the infinite variety of expression of which he is capable.[100] Sin is described as a state in which there occurs a rupture of this essential relationship. Man in exaggerating his freedom displaces himself from his position of finitude in regard to what is eternal. It is man's very freedom that paradoxically provides both for the possibility of creativity as well as estrangement from the Divine described as follows:

> The state of our whole life is estrangement from others and ourselves because we are estranged from the ground of our being because we are estranged from the origin and aim of our life. And we do not know where we have come from or where we are going.[101]

It is this state of estrangement or separation that we refer to as sin.

In a similar vein, it has been suggested that sin is the "refusal to admit finiteness" [102] in spite of man's evident ability to recognize his finitude. And furthermore, that "it is not his finiteness, dependence, and weakness but his anxiety about it that tempts him to sin." [103] Anxiety becomes therefore the internal precondition of sin. Sin is man's unwillingness to acknowledge his creatureliness and dependence upon God and his ensuing effort to make his own life independent and secure. Sin, in other words, is a pretension by man of being more than he is.

Sin may be yet characterized as man's unwillingness to adjust his life to the mystery and grandeur of existence.[104] He seeks refuge from finiteness—from his helplessness in the face of Time—by conquering and controlling Space. Man attempts to distract himself from his anxieties and insecurities in regard to Time in his preoccupation with the conquest of Space. In a word:

> Man's sin is in his failure to live what he is. Being master of the earth, man forgets that he is the servant of God.[105]

Whether it be sin or neurosis, I wish to emphasize that we are concerned with man's actions rather than his substance. From the perspective of sin man exaggerates and perverts his freedom; he seeks to become powerful and dominant; he assumes the unequivocal position of "I am"; he sees only his boldness. From the perspective of neurosis it is by means of tactics of powerlessness and submissiveness that man seeks to preserve his "self" esteem. He assumes the position of "I am not"; he is overmodest. The ensuing estrangement of man whether in the form of sin or neurosis—master or slave—is based on his inclination toward self-love*: it inevitably insinuates itself into all his actions. Prior to a further consideration of the problem of self-love, estrangement, or separation as revealed in sin and neurosis, let us briefly touch upon the social dimension relevant to our discussion.

SIN AND THE SOCIAL ORDER

The view of sin, portrayed above as separation or self-sufficiency leading toward the narrowing of existence, is manifest not only in individual action but within the social institutions wherein man's actions take place. From a theological perspective, how then do social structures reflect man's estrangement (sin)? It is, as an example, our secular notion of progress that becomes an expression of the self-sufficiency characteristic of capitalistic society:

---

* It may also be said that whereas the neurotic's strategy leads him to a position in which he believes he is "nothing" that of the sinner defines him as "everything." Both positions, as we shall see, are in reality strategies towards indulgence in self-love.

We come out of a time in which existence was directed toward itself in which the forms of life were self-sufficient and closed against the invasions of the eternal.[106]

A further allusion to the self-sufficiency as well as the presumptuousness of man is that he

> . . . has lost the reality of creation in his concepts of evolution that of revelation in the theory of the unconscious and that of redemption in the setting up of social or national goals.[107]

It is here intimated that man has lost contact with the origin and goal of the world. The appeal of nationalism may become a pretext whereby the anxiety of confrontation with the meaning of existence is avoided. The exorbitant cost of pursuing nationalistic pretense is manifest in the cataclysmic upsurges of collectivism on one hand and rampant individualism on the other that is characteristic of the modern-day era.

SELF-LOVE: SIN

What are the further ramifications of this state of separation that we have now noted in both the individual and social dimensions of existence? This state of estrangement fostered by the anxieties of Time renders man more exquisitely aware of his powerlessness, isolation, and loss of meaning. He now has the realization that the source of power lies beyond his grasp. The reliance of his "self" on universal meaning, his dependence on that which gives ultimate independence, his relation to that which is eternal has become compromised. He is no longer able to submit to a higher order of meaning and morality in order that he acquire the necessary courage to minimize the anguish of self-love and estrangement.

There are no longer any acknowledged norms beyond himself. Essentially, he has lost his belief in "Thou art, therefore I am." [108] In an attempt to regain his foothold man proceeds to establish himself independently—to exaggerate his self-love; his individualism comes to the fore; his personal needs become his paramount concern. This leads to the unchecked expression of vital desires; desires for which standards of perfection are absent. Man, in short, becomes the measure of all things. He believes himself able to live without any limitations whatsoever aside from the fulfillment of his proper needs; herein the condition of sin is epitomized. The mass man of today is such an individual:

> This contentment with himself leads him to shut himself off from any external court of appeal. Not to listen nor to submit his opinions to judgment. Not to consider others' existence. His intimate feeling of power urges him always to exercise predominance. He will act then as if he and his life were the only things existing in the world and consequently will intervene in all matters imposing his own vulgar views without respect or regard of others without limit or reserve, that is to say in accordance with the system of direct action.[109]

Paradoxically, the more man devotes himself to his personal existence and needs the more aware he becomes of his insignificance in relation to the universe. His entire being is permeated by doubt as he senses the finite transitory conditional nature of his existence. Ultimately, the more consideration he has given to his own immediate necessities the more he senses his isolation and insecurity. Thus self-aggrandizement serves to heighten his sense of anxiety rather than minimize it. His independence and self-sufficiency in turn aggravate his sense of estrangement. In this condition of sin, rather than resolving, man ironically becomes more vulnerable to the ultimate problems of existence—those of meaninglessness, guilt, and death. How does he cope with this predicament of existential vulnerability and insecurity?

COLLECTIVISTIC SOLUTIONS

The predicament is one of a lack of purpose, meaning, and direction that is a consequence of intensified self-interest which in turn is an outcome of man's sense of insignificance in the face of his existential dilemmas. He thus loses his bearing and his standards fall by the wayside. His position becomes further falsified as he becomes blinded to destiny and deaf to any appeal. Man is disarmed as he loses awareness of transcendental laws that could have served him as a guide for his action. In spite of these demands of existence he sees no alternative but to persist in considering the universe as having the sole purpose of satisfying his needs.

One possible solution of this crisis is to seek out the refuge of the collective within which one is able to conceal his claims to personal existence and self-interest and thereby attempt to alleviate the anxiety of his pretentiousness. The mass man confounds his egoistic interests with the supposed noble enterprise of the collective. The ideology and slogans of the collective thus conceal the partial perspective of its vested interest groups. No collective admits to its base aims that are cloaked by its pretense of concern for universal virtues of peace and justice. Collective pride and ideology thereby effectively conceal the contingencies and precariousness of man's claims to personal existence. Man thus attempts to assure his life of significance beyond itself through participation in collectivistic enterprises and thereby attempts to minimize the anxieties of his tenuous existence. Yet at the same time cloaked by collectivistic pretense he believes that he is able to persist unabated in his egoistic and self-centered pursuits.

The collective thereby effectively compensates for the yawning abyss of a meaningless existence. It serves to narrow the gaze of its members and thereby fend off the anxiety of insignificance. The collective in its supposed noble pursuits seeks to counter the anxiety of existence and yet promote its particular interests by forging a sense of unity, purpose, and cohesion:

> In nations as in children reason seeks unity in all things. Simplicity, uniformity, identity, and hierarchy as well as size and mass.[110]

The collective thereby provides the simplicity and conformity necessary to quell anxiety and a sense of insignificance.

It in fact provides for an all-pervasive sense of conformity:

In almost all, a homogeneous mass weighs on public authority and crushes down, annihilates every opposing group. The mass —who would credit it as one sees its compact multitudinous appearance?—does not wish to share life with those who are not of it. It has a deadly hatred of all that is not itself.[111]

Thus man, as can be expected, pays a high price for his purchase of meaning and purpose from the collective. He barters meaning in return for submission and servitude. As in the individual dimension of the sadomasochistic relationship he thereby loses the possibility of confirmation as a unique individual. The collective only knows man as a part; man becomes unable to act; he is simply acted upon.

SELF-LOVE: NEUROSIS

I have described the human situation as one in which man is threatened by the ultimate problems of existence, as a consequence of which he resorts to more drastic efforts at self-aggrandizement as well as an intensified pursuit of self-interest. It is this condition of self-sufficiency and separation that has been called *sin*. It is ironically one in which man is more thoroughly exposed to the fundamental human anxieties of guilt, meaninglessness, and death.

The individual who is unable or unwilling to allay his anxieties by total submergence to the all-embraciveness of the collective seeks other means of resolving this human crisis. Individual neurotic strategies are such means. They are characterized by a similar quest for certainty, acceptance, and consensus in order to allay the difficulties of the situation. It is through the use of tactics of coercion and power (Chapter 6), as in the case of Mrs. H., that the neurotic individual in his relations with others seeks to assuage his sense of insignificance in the face of life.

This struggle for power and acceptance that characterizes neurotic interaction must be comprehended not as a playing out of "intra-psychic" conflict or as simply a product of oppressive social circumstances. The indulgence in neurotic power tactics is a concerted attempt to nullify the effects of his retreat in the face of the three-fold anxieties of existence. It is a quest for certainty, acceptance, conformity, and consensus to be achieved by means of coercion and manipulation principally through tactics of submission* and as such becomes a convenient distraction from the anguish and terror of existence. Each partner thereby attempts to shield himself from the demands of existence by believing that its solution lies in the coercion of his interlocutor. Each uses the other in order that his gaze be screened and shielded from the radical, harsh realities of existence. As an outcome of such manipulation of his interlocutor the neurotic hopes to provide for himself a semblance of order, purpose, and meaning.

Having described neurotic strategies, at this point I wish to comment on the correlation between the more classical neurotic symptoms such as phobias, obsessions, depressions, and the problem of human existence in its totality. It must be clear that the despair and anguish of which the patient complains is not the result of such symptoms but rather are the reasons for their existence. It is in fact these very symptoms that shield him from the torment of the profound contradictions that lie at the heart of human existence. The particular phobia or obsession is the very means by which man who lives in this paradoxical situation eases the burden of his life's tasks. It is by means of his symptoms that he is able to justify his neurotic tactics (Chapter 6, IV) by which he is able to conceal his coercive quest for acceptance, maintain his pride, and what is most important, assuage his sense of insignificance.

Such tactics do not in themselves suffice to shield man from the demands placed upon him by the problems of life. He must further attempt to simplify the perplexities of the human situation. Thus, neurotic symptoms serve to reduce and narrow—to magically transform the world so that he may be distracted from his concerns of death, guilt, and meaninglessness. The neurotic preoccupied with his symptom is lead to believe that

* The patient herein assumes the position of "I am not" or "nothing." As such he believes he is able to eschew responsibility in the face of life's problems and yet secure recognition or acceptance.

his central task is one of confrontation with his particular obsession or phobia. In a sense his neurosis allows him to take control of his destiny—to transform the whole of life's meaning into the simplified meaning emanating from his self-created world.

His particular thoughts (phobias or obsessions) become ends in themselves. As in the collective within which man remains open solely to the appeal of its aims and ends, so the neurotic symptom becomes for the individual his sole source of appeal. The demands of existence are thereby thought to be excluded as the neurotic loses himself in the labyrinthic maze of his obsessive thought. Thoughts no longer serve the purpose of fulfilling and evaluating the totality of one's commitment but become the very means of escaping responsibility for such commitment.

Ironically, it is in this reduced unambiguous world of his own creation that man persists in the illusion that his neurotic deception will yet enable him to by-pass the demands of existence. Unfortunately, the neurotic is not in a position to realize that in spite of the price he is willing to pay in suffering and misery—and no matter the extent to which he labors to create convincing deceptions—the demands of life are inescapable. The full meaning of this dilemma is depicted as follows:

> Pathological anxiety leads to self-affirmation on a limited fixed and unrealistic basis and to a compulsory defense of this basis. Pathological anxiety in relation to the anxiety of fate and death produces an unrealistic security; in relation to the anxiety of guilt and condemnation, an unrealistic perfection; in relation to the anxiety of doubt and meaninglessness and unrealistic certitude.[112]

In more succinct terms:

> Neurosis is the way of avoiding non-being by avoiding being.[113]

Neurotic strategies are therefore merely pseudosolutions that compound and aggravate the original crisis which they were meant to resolve.

We have now come full circle: the self-sufficiency, pseudo-power, and pretentiousness of man estranged from his world have been characterized as sin. The profound contradictions and anxieties of existence have led to the condition of sin on one hand and neurotic strategies on the other in an attempt to resolve this crisis. Neurotic conduct similarly fails to resolve the crisis of this situation as it itself remains an expression—albeit in the concealed form of powerlessness—of man's self-sufficiency and self-love snugly set within the confines of a self-styled world. It is the basic similarity between these two modes of conduct—sin and neurosis—that has been designated by the term sin-neurotic complex; the former in which man exaggerates his freedom the latter in which he denies it. Both are forms of self-love, a strategy whereby man seeks to hide from the realities of existence.

SIN, NEUROSIS, AND EVERY-DAY LIFE

It would have been quite erroneous to imply that the deception and concealment in the context described above is limited merely to what some may consider the "extraordinary" condition of either sin or neurosis. To the contrary, man as a fictional flimsy animal is continually faced with the temptation to hide. We may therefore expect concealment and deception in regard to the problems of existence to characterize ordinary, every-day human conduct.

The roles, duties, and responsibilities of the individual child are originally donned in his effort to maintain his self-esteem in the face of parental and social authority. The adult role of worker, politician, soldier, and so forth, not only provides for the efficient functioning of the social order but also offers refuge and solace from the demands and perplexities of existence.

Philosophers of the stature of Kierkegaard and Nietzsche[114] have expounded on the manner in which, for example, the common every-day pursuits of knowledge may alienate man from himself and plunge him into an anonymous world of generalization and convention. The disciplines of learning in effect have helped to create an artificial world in which man shuns, to his own detriment, the radical realities of existence that are nevertheless inescapable.

The general falsity of every-day life is nowhere better portrayed than in Tolstoi's story[115] about the death of an ordinary man in which are depicted the means by which the common social niceties, ambitions, and customs serve as vehicles by which one may veer from the realities of existence. He says of the main character, Ivan:

> Even when he was at the School of Law he was just what he remained for the rest of his life: a capable, cheerful, good natured, and sociable man, though strict in the fulfillment of what he considered to be his duty: and he considered his duty to be what was so considered by those in authority.

Later, in the story, we are witness to the thoughts of Ivan who is reviewing the events of his lifetime while lying on his death bed:

> It occurred to him that . . . his professional duties, and the whole arrangement of his life and of his family, and all his social and official interests, might all have been false—all that for which he had lived—was not real at all, but a terrible and huge deception which had hidden both life and death.

Is it not the very dilemma of Tolstoi's Ivan—anguish in regard to the meaning of one's personal existence—that the neurotic seeks to avoid in the creation of his unambiguous self-styled world?

Both sin and neurosis may therefore be conceptualized as particular modes of conduct by which one attempts to hide from the oppressive demands of existence. The former is characterized by a desperate quest for power through efforts at self-aggrandizement and self-sufficiency. The latter is characterized by a perpetual escape from the demands of existence by seeking refuge in the unambiguity and pseudosafety of the neurotic's powerless condition. Thus man's life as we have described it is too often linked to his efforts to resolve the demands of existence through one means of retreat or another.

I have thus far signaled man's escape from freedom and responsibility and as such his inevitable losing battle with life, as it is manifested in regard to the individual social and existential dimensions. Is in fact man simply condemned to withdraw and retreat from the exigencies of existence? Or are there yet alternatives that may be ennobling to the grand possibilities that lie within man? It is to a discussion of alternative modes of conduct, without which the resolution of the problems of sin and neurosis is merely wishful thinking, that may offer man hope to fulfill more fruitfully the possibilities of his existence that I now turn.

FREEDOM AND HUMANISTIC

PSYCHOTHERAPY

--- *Chapter 9*

The psychotherapeutic encounter ought to offer one possibility, amongst others, by which the individual may free himself to become integrated into the larger community of men. This requires that he reject the ways of powerlessness and helplessness created by his long-standing retreat from the challenge of having to make meaningful choices and decisions. It is this very powerlessness, as I have indicated, that in fact lies at the heart of the neurotic way of life and is concealed, disguised, and exploited by means of neurotic symptoms.

The basic supposition of a humanistic psychotherapy is that free choice rather than compulsion and constraint is a possibility for all. Man does not have to be tomorrow what he is today. It is not the inability to choose, per se, that distinguishes the neurotic from the so-called normal. It is simply that the former has made the kinds of choices that have humiliated and constrained him in his life situation. He has become what he has made of himself. The humanistic therapist acknowledges that man has been victimized and trapped by his way of life rather than by his biological heritage. As the suffering of the neurotic is the outcome of his mistaken and unfortunate choices, psychotherapy must focus on the origin, meaning, and consequences of these very choices.

Humanistic psychotherapy cannot offer man a new way of life; it may only allow the patient the opportunity to examine the implications of his life as he is living it and thereupon give consideration to alternative modes of living. Psychoanalysis was, of course, never meant to be a philosophy of life but rather an impartial tool designed to enlighten the patient as to the meaning of his actions, feelings, and thoughts so that he might be able to broaden his narrowed existence by means of wiser, more fruitful choices. If the meaning of ethics is to prompt man to question his actions, then psychotherapy as an inquiry into neurotic conduct, one variety of human action, is necessarily an ethical discipline par excellence.

Neurosis has thus far been portrayed as basically an escape from freedom. It follows that a major task of therapy is to enlighten the patient as to whether or not his actions are based on free involvement. The persistent pursuit of the ways of depression, anxiety, anger, and so forth, indicates simply that the patient is unwilling to embark upon modes of conduct other than those linked to coercive strategies. The consequences and meaning of such refusal must be thoroughly dwelt upon during the course of psychotherapy. Psychotherapy must therefore hold at least the promise that the risk of freedom is more fruitful than its avoidance. The patient must be in a position to corroborate this fundamental fact through appeal to a singularly important piece of evidence—his life experience.

My comments in the preceding chapters have, I hope, persuasively pointed to the pitfalls that exist within a mechanistic deterministic theory of human conduct which I believe characterizes psychoanalysis, a theory based necessarily on a conceptualization of the psychiatric symptom as a product of mechanistic instinctual causes. It is a notion that has ironically lent a strong impetus to prevailing psychiatric practice of the day, utilizing to a large extent mechanistic objectifying techniques such as drugs, behavioral conditioning, and shock treatment. These techniques in their turn reflect the underlying assumption of the user that patient conduct is an outcome of internal causes beyond his control and responsibility. The patient engaged in these treatment modalities becomes an object of manipulation in which the question of responsibility and subjectivity is subordinated to the more immediate goal of achieving a "cure" by means of active physical intervention.

In spite of the implications of its theory, the practice of classical psychoanalysis (as well as psychotherapy in general) is at least implicitly concerned with the freedom, spontaneity, and responsibility of the patient. This is, as I shall note in more detail below, made manifest by the tendency to emphasize the patient's responsibility in such matters as financial obligation for missed sessions, discouragement of collateral involvement, mutuality in regard to termination, free association, and so forth.

The purpose of this chapter is to suggest a format by which the humanistic dimension may be incorporated as central rather than merely incidental to the practice of psychotherapy so that it may be consistent with our theory of human conduct indicated throughout this work. The ceaseless task of unfolding issues of freedom, choice, and meaning is essential to the notion of humanism; it provides the crucial link between a theory of neurosis and practice of psychotherapy.

Lest the practice of psychotherapy be inconsistent with the spirit of our humanistic orientation, it will be necessary that a degree of caution, restraint, and care be exercised in the therapeutic situation as suggested by the saying:

> Thou hast been set as a dam to save the poor man from drowning, but behold thou art thyself the flood.

Thus the therapist must take care that by his actions he does not compound and aggravate the difficulties (interpersonal, social, and existential) that already hamper the exercise of freedom and responsibility which lie at the heart of the patient's suffering.

The central motif of therapy must stem from an idealistic notion suggested by Adler—anyone can do anything—and thus the patient has the possibility to be freer than he is. The limitation of man's freedom is not at all based on the existence of instincts, repressed feelings, unwanted thoughts, but rather it is his actions or plan of life that enslaves him.

One who acts helpless becomes helpless. One has not only become helpless but has staked his entire pride and meaning on an existence of helplessness. Resistance then becomes the tactic and the means by which the patient seeks, to avoid the unfamiliarity and anguish of freedom. The refusal to acknowledge the possibility of freedom is in fact what remains conveniently unconscious. By clinging tenaciously to his symptoms the patient seeks to justify his way of powerlessness and thereby enables himself to postpone the task of accepting the risks and unfamiliarity of freedom and responsibility. The work of therapy is basically an inquiry into the meaning of man's existence in order to render the patient aware of the significance and consequences of such postponement.

The task of the therapist is then to encourage analysis of the patient's life situation, not simply for the sake of understanding but rather in the interests of his self-liberation. Conversely it must be realized that attempts at intervention, control, and domination by the therapist make analysis and inquiry superfluous as well as hindering the patient's efforts in the direction of self-liberation. The patient who may desire such intervention in the interest of justifying his helplessness may now attempt to falsify his position in order to win the favor of the therapist. A mechanistic-causal theory of neurosis postulating forces beyond the patient's control tends to foster and promote such authoritative intervention. The resulting falsity obviously vitiates the task of inquiry and compounds the inclination toward retreat and escape for which the patient originally sought the services of the therapist.

Further, intervention and coercion unwittingly communicate to the patient his basic incapacity for self-reliance. Instruction, advice, and direct counseling on how to live one's life are often denigrating, and antithetical to the needs of self-liberation, as they may signal to the patient that he is powerless and must forever remain so. He becomes all the more convinced that he must continue to resort to "seeming" rather than to "being" (neurotic strategies represent the effort to avoid the risks of living by "seeming" rather than "being") as all his efforts towards self-reliance are subtly discounted. If the therapist is not to coerce the patient by means of unmindful authoritarian imposition, he is left with the other more arduous alternative of attempting to influence him to become what he can.

The therapist must at all times realize that the material brought forth by the patient is a product of their relationship. The therapist is not simply a passive agent that allows the patient a catharsis as a midwife delivers a baby. The analysis of transference as well as the resolution of the Oedipal complex (as already described in terms of a power struggle) involves bringing to the patient's awareness his persistent appeal to "authoritarian archaic objects and rules." [116] In this regard, continuing caution must be exercised so that the therapist does not become a parental surrogate. Otherwise, any consequent intervention, imposition, and control exercised by the therapist is likely to foster antagonism that readily serves the patient as a distraction from the necessary scrutiny of his life. When given the opportunity he is easily enticed into a convenient preoccupation with the therapist.

The effectiveness of the therapist is a measure of his inclination to exercise carefulness rather than care. He must offer assistance rather than his self; he ought to be concerned rather than attempt to control. Only in this manner does he allow for the possibility of emancipating the patient from the forces that otherwise bind him to the therapist.

To minimize intervention a contractural model of therapy has been proposed.[117] The contract becomes the ground rules upon which therapy is conducted. It provides at least verbal agreement to insure that the therapist neither dominates nor is dominated by his patient. The fruitfulness of therapy in this regard depends on whether or not the patient views his involvement as one based on choice or necessity. The latter case is obviously linked to coercive strategies and serves only to perpetuate rather than resolve the patient's dilemma. It is therefore not at all ironical that therapy becomes a means towards the liberation of the patient only if the liberty of the therapist is given equal consideration.

If, as implied all along, neurosis is basically a renunciation of man's responsibility to be free, the psychotherapeutic contract serves to redirect the patient toward the path of his liberation. The adherence to the psychotherapeutic contract accentuates the therapist's efforts to render his patient aware of his manifold tactics that delay and postpone his quest for freedom. As such the responsibility called for in adherence to the contract communicates to the patient that autonomous conduct can become one of the avenues of life realistically open to him.*

Failure of therapy may stem from inadequate or insufficient information imparted to the patient. The therapist may further lack competence as an educator or serve as an ineffective model and thereby impede the patient in his effort to seek alternative modes of conduct. The patient's understanding of his life situation emanates not only from the verbal communications of the therapist but, what is even more important, from his actions and conduct within the therapeutic setting: the instructor is more significant than the instruction. The therapist who eschews intervention both confronts the patient and enables him to significantly comprehend his basic problem—the evasion of responsibility. The patient now unable to rely on intervention by the therapist is obliged to experience and fulfill his own potential in the direction of self-reliance. He comes to the realization that *he himself is his best servant.*

THE TASK OF THE PATIENT

The patient, for his part, if he is to become involved in psychotherapy, must be willing to explore the meaning and purpose of his symptoms. He must be inclined toward the idea that his symptom is not the cause of his difficulties in living but rather its consequence. Thus the patient's way of life rather than the symptom becomes the focus of therapy. The symptom,

---

* The contract as spelled out by Szasz proscribes intervention either for or against the interests of the patient.

understood as a consequence of the patient's way of life, is central rather than accidental to it. This concept distinguishes perhaps most clearly the medical from the psychological symptom: the medical symptom always refers to an organ, the psychological symptom to the organism—man.

The patient, ironically, becomes aware of the significance of his symptom only if he is willing to look beyond it—not to its cause, but to its meaning in so far as his life is concerned. The more profound the patient's preoccupation with the symptom itself the more difficult will it be to resolve, if at all. How would life be, was Adler's question to the patient, if you were rid of your particular phobia, depression, or obsession?[118] The problem signaled as an answer to such a hypothetical question provides the beginning text of an inquiry into the patient's life situation. In the patient who does not envision any such problems, psychotherapy in the strict sense of the word is precluded. Why? The patient in denying the existence of problems beyond his symptom chooses to view it as accidental rather than as a purposeful tactic to obscure the relevant difficulties of his life situation.

It is the meaning of the symptom in this light that remains unconscious, for only when unconscious does it allow the patient to pursue his project, aims, and goals—his misguided life plan. The accompanying shame, suffering, guilt, misery, and so forth, are not sufficient reasons to seek resolution of the symptom. This is understandable when it is realized that it is the symptom and the accompanying affects that allow him to secure his goals, wants, and desires—those of retreat and at the same time acceptance. Suffering then is not necessarily a motive for sincere involvements in therapy, but simply the means with which to pursue one's unfortunate plan of action more tenaciously.

It therefore becomes an essential task of therapy to clarify for the patient the details of his life plan. He must strive to realize that his way of life conflicts with the demands of reality; and at the same time he becomes aware that his symptom, although clearly disconcerting, simply enables him to maintain his face and self-esteem while both concealing and pursuing his unproductive life plan. Only this realization will tempt the patient to seek new avenues of conduct, to redefine himself and create for himself new choices. He must realize that the underlying task of doing away with his symptom involves nothing less than becoming someone *other than himself*. For it is his habitual life plan of withdrawal, hesitation, and powerlessness which forms the raison d'être of his symptom. Once he has seized upon this realization, only two simple alternatives arise: he may remain committed to his accustomed pseudosecure old ways, or seek to meet the risk and challenge of recouping and exercising the power that he has managed unwittingly to forfeit.

A thorough understanding of one's life situation becomes a reality only as he is able to entertain the possibility of embarking upon new avenues of conduct. He can truly afford the luxury of understanding the profound meaning of symptoms such as inferiority feelings, depression, and guilt only as he can afford to do without them. Paradoxically, in order to comprehend fully his burdensome way of life he must be prepared to abandon it. The degree of significant understanding of one's constricting situation is therefore inseparable from the possibilities of a freer existence.

One must literally work himself over if he is fully to understand as well as to do without the symptoms and difficulties that have plagued him. To do this, the patient must have accepted the fact that he has not lived his life as he ought to have done, and therefore he must be prepared to consider alternatives. He must remain true to his intent to live more dynamically rather than remain in his perceptual state of neurotic stagnation. Dynamic movement becomes necessary if he is to recapture both the power and destiny that he has given over to others through years of abdication. Essential to a recouping of this power is that he no longer be afraid to err: he must ground his self-image on deed rather than retreat. Only then will he be prepared to accept the risk of choice, responsibility, and greater freedom.

Notes on Techniques of Psychotherapy with Mrs. H.

At this point it must be noted that the essence of the ground rules for humanistic psychotherapy provides that following the initial trial period the balance of power between patient and therapist remains in the hands of the former. For example, termination of therapy must always be at the discretion of Mrs. H. The fee, ironically, becomes another essential aspect in providing her with a realistic sense of power and control within the therapy situation, which is crucial if the patient is to be able to transcend and ultimately resolve her marked sense of obligation. It is after all her intense feeling of obligation that is instrumental in her perpetual capitulation and acquiescence to the demands of the Other. To pay the therapist is a step toward acquiring the necessary awareness with which to confront her sense of obligation. As a further instance, being held financially responsible for missed sessions nullifies her inclination to seize upon an occasion by which she may flaunt this sense of obligation, heighten her guilt, promote fears of rejection and ultimately create sufficient ground for her "logical" withdrawal from the therapy situation as she has similarly done in her life's circumstances.

Mrs. H. began to cite instances of general anxiety that began, after a period of relative tranquility in her life, to plague her, and which continued to occur. This period may be construed as a transitional phase in which Mrs. H. begins to find that her ways of agreeableness, apology, and general subordination are no longer a necessity but rather a well-designed strategy. To see one's ways as strategies implies that other though perhaps unfamiliar alternatives beckon. These new though unfamiliar possibilities may very well underlie her current anxiety. Further, and yet along these lines, her anxiety reflects the fact that when it becomes no longer necessary to live as she has in the past it is nevertheless impossible to not live at all. If her neurotic strategies were designed so that others have always chosen for her, she must now choose for herself—quite an alien endeavor.

We are not at all surprised to note that with her new-found awareness that it is no longer necessary to her to remain miserable and submissive she becomes concerned and guilt-ridden lest her actions displease her husband. Undoubtedly it is a risk that must be taken into account, a risk, however, that must be considered along with the even higher risks of her habitual enslavement. It also must be made clear that her guilt in this situation may represent yet another strategy by which she hopes to be able to refrain from choosing alternate ways of living—of perpetuating her surrender. In another session Mrs. H., yet more aware of the alternative to that of her perpetual misery, is able to express her discontent at having so long acted as if she were "nothing" but a servant in her own home. She is now able to envision, however minimally, the possibility that she too may have rights and that her word ought to count. She has to this point given power to the word of her husband; why not to those of her own?

The therapist during such a transition period may be tempted: ought one to take steps in the direction of actively assisting or advising Mrs. H. in the matter of, let us say, securing employment that might rapidly enhance her self-esteem? Why not take steps such as consulting with her prospective employer in the interest of aiding Mrs. H. to obtain a position? I believe that the "hands off" policy of the therapist is justified in that any such urging is basically inconsistent with the task of therapy, for several reasons. First, intervening on behalf of Mrs. H. would communicate to her, in contradiction to the implicit message of therapy, that in fact she is helpless to decide and act on her own. If this were to occur Mrs. H. would have accomplished what perhaps unwittingly she has all along sought to demonstrate to both herself and the therapist —her undeniable helplessness. For the therapist to take such action would place him in the position of the salesman who desires to sell Chevrolets and drives away before the eyes of his customer in a shiny new Plymouth. Second, any manifested insistence on the part of the therapist is very likely to promote a sense of obligation or fear of letting down the therapist which Mrs. H. may attempt to exploit as a basis for eventual withdrawal from therapy. Mrs. H. would be most likely to seize upon any such insistence or enthusiasm on the part of the therapist to document her failure to act in accordance with his request, and not wishing to face the risk of incurring his displeasure, would be most likely to terminate therapy and conveniently continue her ways as of old. It is therefore necessary to anticipate that Mrs. H. will have difficulty in committing herself to the therapy situation (as she does in all situations) and it therefore must be left as unfettered as possible. Yet another implication: if the therapist were to assume such a stance he would undoubtedly compound Mrs. H.'s conviction, mistaken as it may be, that she is only able to survive in life by looking toward the Other. The ultimate of this position is her reluctance to act in life unless given recognition and assurance beforehand. The task of therapy is to challenge the assumption that she needs primarily to rely on the acceptance of the Other rather than on her initiative in spite of the fact that the patient may believe it to be tantamount to her destiny. Intervention on the part of the therapist tempts the patient to evade this challenge.

To a large degree, Mrs. H. justifies her strategy of capitulation in that in her eyes to do otherwise would be selfish and ignoble on her part. Is her way of life based on virtue and consideration for the Other? It is evident that this is not the case. Her general attitude of complaint and in specific instances her jealousies in regard to her husband's private secretary would be inconsistent with an attitude based on virtue and selflessness. Her abdication can be clearly seen as a form of blackmail or bribery emanating from a position of powerlessness and therefore one of necessity rather than choice. This is further clarified as she recounts the many arguments she has had with her huband, who is inclined to intimidate and berate her for losing at her favorite game of bingo. In view of this predicament, strategies of coercion and bribery rather than benevolence may well be necessary in order to minimize the power her husband is likely to utilize against her.

Mrs. H. has related during the course of therapy that she has not made herself quite as available to others as in the past. Simultaneously it appears that her state of panic, anxiety, and depression have lessened and now take the more prevalent form of disinterest, lack of enthusiasm, and boredom. Her overall situation is thus neither one of enthusiasm on one hand nor of extreme panic and fright on the other. This state may signal that she is prepared to confront her old ways but as yet is not able fully to transcend them. Her reluctance to embark upon new ways is made manifest during a session in which she poses a question to me as to whether or not she would get "better" if she were to seek and obtain employment. Once again we are witness to her expression of worthlessness in so far as taking risks are based on her very own actions. She yet prefers assurance and recognition prior to embarking upon any such task. This persistent temptation is further reflected in Mrs. H.'s numerous queries to the therapist as to whether or not she ought discontinue her sessions. As therapy represents involvement and possible scrutiny of her performance she persists in her attempts either to withdraw or to receive assurance and recognition rather than risk rejection or rebuff.

Further comments by Mrs. H. as regards our therapy situation reveal her inclination to believe that she will be chastised for either wasting my time or for not progressing sufficiently well in therapy. Here it is important that the ground rules of therapy be once again clarified: namely, that the decision to terminate our sessions remains entirely in the hands of Mrs. H. If this be the case, the question must be posed to her as to what she believes is at stake. In spite of the fact that she may have evidence or may construct evidence and may even conclude rightly that I am dissatisfied with her, it must be repeatedly emphasized that her power to terminate therapy must necessarily overweigh any dissatisfaction that I may have with her. Mrs. H. persistently attempts to withdraw by attempting to suggest that it is I who am bored or perhaps angry with her. Once again Mrs. H.'s intent is to promote my interest and comfort and thereby deny her own. She continues to decide to allow the Other to decide for her; she is *nothing*, the Other *everything*. The consequences and suffering tied to such action are in fact the story of her life. The therapist and the therapy situation must allow her the possibility of pursuing other ways.

It would appear that Mrs. H. is somewhat more aware of this predicament. It is perhaps attested to by her present realization that neighbors have often mocked her for her overindulgence with other people's children and generally being too readily available to satisfy the whims of others and at the same time too modest about her own —all this to the delight of the neighborhood children.

What are the risks of a situation in which her word and deeds are to be taken seriously? (An essential task of therapy is to explore such a possibility.) Along these lines Mrs. H. reiterates her reluctance to seek employment and maintains that the position she has in mind is one in which people were readily fired and this would be too difficult for her to withstand. Thus the risk of believing that her survival is not necessarily tied to the whims of the next person would at this moment be too disconcerting to consider. Mrs. H. has, after all, to this moment counted heavily on relying on others through the unreflective denial of her own powers. Whether or not to abandon these ways would appear to be her struggle for the moment. It is the anguish thereby engendered that prompted Mrs. H. to refuse such a position. In order to further justify her stance of withdrawal Mrs. H. mentions that she will shortly be hospitalized for a thyroid condition. She discusses her extreme panic at the thought of being hospitalized alone and away from her family. Her panic is a further means by which she defines herself as one who cannot survive on her own.

We must at this point take cognizance of the difficulties in general, and those more specifically of Mrs. H., in so far as the matter of safeguarding her interests or claiming her rights is concerned. This fundamental difficulty is made manifest by her apparently paradoxical complaints that having won at bingo she became markedly upset and anxious. It would appear that "winning" and/or "having" is antithetical to her strategy of defining herself as one who "has not" —one who cannot "be" and therefore one who must out of necessity be served and indulged by the Other. If this be her goal—to only win by losing—it is consistent that to win at bingo or to become angry at someone who may seek to exploit her would engender anxiety precisely in order to prompt her to persevere in her familiar stance of appeasement and surrender, a stance perpetually enticing in that it provides the illusion of offering protection against the risk of incurring the displeasure of the Other. In capitulating she is led to believe that she will win acceptance and with it meaning, order, and convenience from the all-powerful Other. Her way of life, feelings, and thoughts all serve to perpetuate this assumption.

In many ways, Mrs. H. had hoped that to *submit* would mean to conquer. She undoubtedly became involved in psychotherapy when in fact it became clear that to *submit* meant to be *conquered* in turn. The therapy situation must offer at least an alternative—one in which she is neither the exploiter nor exploited—one in which the struggle for self-emancipation is an authentic option. She must *alter* rather than *accept* her oppressive situation.

CONCLUSION

If psychotherapy is to be an efficacious instrument of liberation, there must be established a degree of consistency between the theory it presupposes and the techniques it utilizes. The patient's suffering is considered an outcome as well as an expression of a purposeful life plan centered on a stance of powerlessness. Accordingly, psychotherapy must provide for a thorough clarification of the full consequences of this strategy. Further, active intervention or manipulation ought to be eschewed so as not inadvertently to compound the patient's plight of powerlessness. The therapist must take care to influence the patient to become what he wants to be rather than impose upon him. The stance of the therapist conveys an over-all perspective to the patient by which he may create new possibilities for the future rather than be sunk in the despair of what he has considered to be an unalterable heritage of the past. Neither the theory nor practice of psychotherapy ought inadvertently to place limitations upon the patient's possibilities to be free.

COMMUNITY AND FAITH

Chapter 10

TOWARD SOCIAL RECONSTRUCTION

Psychotherapy has been shown to concern itself with the individual's qua individual problem of freedom, responsibility, and choice. The curtailment of one's rights as seen in the human condition of neurosis, alienation, and sin makes it necessary that we be concerned as well with the social dimensions of this problem. If man has both a duty and right not to surrender his freedom, it behooves us to investigate and confront the social structures that lead toward this surrender. After all,

> The nature of man is written in capital letters in the nature of the state.[119]

The plight of the individual and his lost freedom is only a microcosmic portrayal of the human condition writ large. This has already been implied by our view that the existence and prevalence of mental illness in itself is a living critique of our democratic heritage.* If one man is not free, no one is. What

---

* In this regard mental illness refers not to an accidental sickness but to powerless people and therefore suffering from the consequences of oppression as do the Blacks, Jews, workers, colonized, and so forth. As such

changes in the social order facilitate man's attempt to become himself? The answer to such a problem is undoubtedly difficult. It will not, however, even be an issue for contemporary psychiatry to consider unless the proper questions are asked. It is in order to remain in a position to ask these questions that we must persist in our effort to recast the language of psychiatry from a mechanistic one reducible to physical dimensions and which thereby ultimately calls for laboratory investigation to a humanistic one focusing on socially useful and purposeful knowledge. Toward this end I have suggested that the restriction of man's action—witness mental illness—has its origins not with what is inside man but in the oppression and violence inflicted upon man by man. With this as our cue we must unceasingly focus on the social structures and institutions through which such repression is glaringly perpetuated.

Neurosis may thus be envisioned not as a product of instinctual endowment but as a protest against the harshness of life's experience; a protest more specifically against the violence and injustice brought to bear against the person of man. If this be the case, then it becomes an imperative task of psychiatry to point to the means with which to curb the unruly forces of chaos, violence, and irrationality which lie within the social structure, and thereby to facilitate man's effort to resolve the problems ensuing from his flight from freedom, whatever form it may take.

To proceed thus, the plight of the psychiatric patient in this regard must be interpreted by reference to oppressive social conditions as is that of the more clearly defined, but similarly humiliated, minority groups. The sufferings of neither one nor the other is accountable in terms of biological make-up.

> Below the corporeal schema I had sketched a historico-radical schema. The elements that I used had been provided for me not by residual sensations and perceptions primarily of a tactile, vestibular, kinesthetic, and visual character, but by the other, the

---

it is exciting to believe that the resolution of the problem of mental illness is inevitably linked to the perpetual and perennial struggle for freedom—an ideal and vision that ought become part of the heritage of psychiatry.

white man, who had woven me out of a thousand details, anec-
dotes, stories. I thought that what I had in hand was to construct a physiological self, to balance space, to localize sensations, and here I was called on *for more*.[120]

The task of contemporary psychiatry calls for far more than the
ceaseless familiar, time-worn efforts of laboratory studies inclined to investigate the physical insides of man. Our concern
must focus instead upon the very fabric of our society that
spews out masses of idiosyncratically (neurotic) oppressed
people as well as those who bear their suffering in more conventional manners—as an instance, the black minority.
Whether it be the downtrodden misery of the black man or of
the neurotic, both have similar social origins and psychiatry
must fulfill its part in discerning and exposing the structures of
our social order which foster man's fallen condition.

THE PROBLEM OF COLLECTIVISM

The human phenomena of neurosis and psychosis exemplify
man's failure or refusal to meet the challenge of existence. Various facets of man's retreat have been touched upon previously
in this work, such as the apathy or violence manifested by oppressed minority groups, as well as those modes of conduct described under the more comprehensive headings of sin and
alienation. It has been a fundamental task of this work to suggest that these modes of conduct do not have their origins in
any innate differences between one person and the next but
merely refer to the manifold ways in which man may lose his
humanity.

These modes of conduct are linked in part to the unruly
forces of contemporary society, inevitably an outcome of our
industrial-technological collective social order geared to specialization, compartmentalization, and anonymity. It is the
constellation of forces arising from this situation that incline
man to retreat from his responsibilities of freedom and choice.
Such retreat is manifested by and leads to retreat from the
problems of responsible decision and choice on the part of the

public and it seriously threatens the traditions of our democratic heritage. Such a democratic heritage must always be based on the ability of a responsible public to exercise a measure of control over the social order to which it has become subject.

> Democracy implies that those vitally affected by any decision men make have an effective voice in that decision. This in turn means that all power to make such a decision be publicly legitimated and that the makers of such decision be held publicly accountable.[121]

In our age it is the technological and managerial expert, complacency, irresponsibility, and oppression (neurotic strategies embody this condition within the interpersonal sphere) that replace a knowledgeable responsible public which is so necessary if the conditions of a genuine democracy are to be realized.

If these conditions are to be achieved the way must be consistent with the goal. The top-heavy power of bureaucracy in the military, industrial, and governmental spheres based upon an affluent middle class must be made more socially responsible. In the process of augmenting the scope of social responsiveness the very structure of society is inevitably reformed. Furthermore, if the means of authentic democracy is to be realized it must involve the restoring of the balance between centralism and decentralism. In a word, a shift from a government from "above" to that of a government from "below" must be inaugurated.

> It is in the interest of the self-constituting society to strive for a continuous change in the nature of power, to that end the government should as much as possible turn to administration . . . efforts must be renewed again and again to determine in what spheres it is possible to alter the ratio between governmental and administrative control in favor of the latter.[122]

The vital decisions of government must come from "below" leaving only the administrative functions to be carried out from "above."

We must work toward the dismantling of the centralized collective and in its place the creation of the ideal community. It is within the former that we have witnessed man's withdrawal from his duty to stand up both justly and truthfully. It is in the development of the latter—the spirit of community that offers man the possibility of becoming himself and with it the decline of alienation and mental illness.

THE PROBLEM OF COMMUNITY

The creation of an ideal community must serve as the model for social reconstruction that is necessary if we are to halt the inimical forces of centralization. The progression toward centralization must be curtailed if man is to receive the confirmation so necessary from the Other if he is to be free and able to realize his potential. The ideal of decentralized communities is the means to this end.

The decentralist tendencies needed for social reconstruction are also necessary to provide man with a sense of communal living. It is within such communal living that he is able to be confirmed by others with whom he lives and works. Social restructuring in the direction of decentralism and community provides man with total integration so necessary if he is to utilize and realize his powers to the fullest. It is in the distance, anonymity, and isolation of a fully centralized social order in which the seeds of abdication, oppression, and powerlessness have been sown.

Community based on integration rather than on specialization—self-government rather than representation—allows its members to take steps towards the reassumption of their powers and responsibilities. It is within decentralized units of living that man is able to fulfill his potential shielded from the isolation and anonymity of the collective. In smaller associative units managed from below man now has the possibility of realizing himself. It is in community, in unity with others, that oppression and estrangement will be overcome so that man may be integrated and recognized as an existing Other. Integration, recognition, and confirmation must be provided by the social order; meaningful choice and decision are otherwise not possible and one outcome, as has been noted, is the existence of mental illness.

Confirmation, the overcoming of otherness, may only be accomplished when man devotes himself to a cause in common with his fellow man. Decentralist communal tendencies provide the setting in which man may have the possibility of becoming devoted to a cause beyond himself. Devotion and commitment by way of communal action are necessary to unite man with his neighbor. After all, as has been said by Ortega y Gasset, men are meant to do things together rather than simply be together.

It is in a common struggle toward a common purpose rather than simply the waving of banners, the mouthing or the chanting of slogans and songs, that bring men together. Social restructuring that provides a setting for man's true and intimate devotion to a cause becomes a necessary step in man's reintegration. It is dedication to such a cause outside oneself that overcomes the basic conflict between conformity and self-will, love and self-love, freedom and unity. A communal cause offers direction and meaning that is crucial if freedom is to be exercised. Otherwise man turns about himself in an aimless and endless labyrinthic maze. The existence of the phenomenon of mental illness is the logical extension of this condition and must be taken as an indication of the distraction, powerlessness, and loss of self to which man easily becomes prey.

Can man be totally integrated within such an idealized social order? The anguish over loss of direction and meaning cannot be completely overcome nor can purpose be fully vitalized till man has the full awareness

> . . . that neither he or his nation can be the end of history and that he does not transcend himself enough to see the end of existence except by faith.[123]

Neither man nor a nation may be an end in itself, only a part of a greater all-embracing structure. I now proceed to a discussion of the necessity and significance of man's relation to Time and Eternity, as he may take neither himself nor his social order as his ultimate referent.

THE EXISTENTIAL DIMENSION

Questions and Answers

I have previously indicated the feasibility of drawing analogies between the concept of sin and that of neurosis. I insisted upon the parallel between sin and neurosis rather than one between neurosis and sickness in the traditional medical sense. For it is the former comparison rather than the latter which allows us to comprehend fully the meaning of the psychiatric symptom. The symptom must point to the totality of the individual's existence—to the meaning of his life—rather than simply to a part of his organism as in the medical approach.

In other terms, I have implied that neurosis and psychosis—conditions that traditionally fall under the domain of psychiatry—are simply manifestations of man's myriad ways of escaping the responsibilities and anguish of his freedom and thereby yielding to oppression. Sin and neurosis are therefore terms to describe man's alienation—ways of living he himself has created that are intended to narrow and simplify the problems of life. Psychiatric symptoms are comparable to sin in that they are both ultimately inseparable from the problem of man's existence. We must turn to the traditional philosophies of life rather than to medicine for their ultimate resolution. This would imply the necessity of attempting a correlation between a philosophy of life such as an ethical discipline or a traditional religion and the core problem that undergirds both the phenomen of sin and of mental illness.

It becomes the task of the science of man, of which psychiatry is an integral discipline, to perpetually question and analyze man's situation. Ceaseless questioning is necessary in order that the relevance between man's predicament and the answers provided by religions and ethical philosophies of life remain actual. The task of psychiatry as part of the science of man is therefore to *query* rather than *prescribe*. At best psychiatry is able to point man in a new direction provided for him by the ethical political or religious disciplines. It must be remembered that psychiatry cannot directly answer the question as to what man ought do with his life nor the related question as to what ought be the meaning of his existence. A humanistic approach to psychiatry enables man to question and be critical of the way he *is* living; implicit in this criticism is that he *ought* live differently.

In so far as psychotherapy is critical of the way man leads his life, it remains simply a method that provides the possibility for the individual to adopt alternate ways of living should he so choose. It is at the point where one comes to realize the devastating consequences of his current way of life that he must, if he is to ameliorate his situation, choose another—perhaps from the various traditional philosophies of life—presenting alternative moralities. Psychotherapy on the individual plane or social reform in communal living may only with much difficulty offer man more ennobling possibilities of living. For the idolatrous self-love in both the individual and social spheres is not easily transcended. In spite of the possibility for elaborate and extensive self-scrutiny man remains encumbered by his partial perspective and by the problems of coercion, power, and violence which ensue from this position. The absence of superordinate meaning compounds this dilemma. Thus man often remains unable to effectively utilize his freedom unless superordinate meaning is incorporated into his existence so that he may withstand the very anguish of freedom. As an instance of such meaning, traditional religion proposes that a covenant between God and man be established. Let us now explore further the notion of superordinate meaning and, what is most important, the price to be paid in its absence.

SELF-SUFFICIENCY

If man is to seek new ways in the direction of enhancing his possibilities of living he must become cognizant of the predicament in which he is ensnared. This predicament has to an extent been characterized by the universal conditions of sin or neurosis. It is the former condition in which man has been revealed as exercising power—power as an end in itself. It is the latter condition that reveals him in the mirror-image condition —man's unwitting aggrandizement and exploitation of his state of powerlessness. Tactics of oppression—both power and powerlessness—lame and hobble man as they are converted into ends or ways of self-sufficiency. It is as such man seeks to protect his prestige and face when confronted with the absence of superordinate meaning possibilities necessary to sustain him.

The exercise of power as well as the submission to it represents man's failure to utilize his freedom—the failure to resolve the perplexities of his existence. Power and powerlessness as embodied in sin and neurosis are strategies of coercion wherein he demands acceptance, consensus, and conformity and they reveal man's inability to alone sustain the risk of his actions, decisions, and choices. These tactics further reveal his indifference, apathy, and retreat from the fact of the fundamental challenges posed by existence. Man thus becomes lost in the triviality and irrelevancy of power tactics as he becomes oblivious to the risk of more noble and higher possibilities. Hence tactics of either power or powerlessness are self-centered or self-sufficient ways by which man attempts to fill the vacuum left by the rejection of religion and other authentic philosophies of life necessary to sustain his pursuit of ennobling endeavors.

It is essentially to bolster himself against the anguish of risk and doubt and the ensuing estrangement and isolation which inclines man towards the stance of self-centeredness and thereupon to his ways of power and coercion. These ways further accentuate differences already existing between men and promote relations based on oppression at one extreme; indifference and apathy at the other. Tactics reducible to a quest for self-sufficiency such as sin and neurosis become the means whereby man attempts to dampen the anguish and risk of confronting the problems of superordinate meaning. However, in attempting to save himself by these means, he loses his humanity by unwittingly excluding consideration of broader possibilities for his fulfillment.

Power and self-sufficiency characterize both the individual and social spheres of existence, expressed by the dictum, "True is what is mine." They are manifested in multifold ways: coercive interpersonal strategies based on submission (neurosis) or domination (sin) as well as the power of collectivistic interest. Generally it is the expression of an age inclined toward expediency in all avenues of life. Thus self-sufficiency, power, and expediency are obviously linked together to enable one to believe that he has been able to conceal his doubts—to negate his uncertainty. It is basically this inability either to confront or eliminate doubt and uncertainty that undergirds the ensuing fanatacism and violence which characterize the modern era. It is perhaps ironical that only when man no longer finds it necessary to seek modes of living that provide refuge from doubt, uncertainty, and insignificance that he will become more human to himself and to his fellow man.

It is the acceptance and awareness of doubt and risk that allow man to look for meaning beyond the limits of his narrowed life.

> As this is the simple truth—that to live is to feel oneself lost—he *who accepts it has* already begun to find himself, to be on firm ground.
>
> He who does not really feel himself lost, is lost without remission; that is to say, he never finds himself, never comes up against his own reality.
>
> The man who discovers a new scientific truth has previously had to smash to atoms almost everything he had learned, and arrives at the new truth with hands bloodstained from the slaughter of a thousand platitudes.[124]

It is only in confronting these limits that he will be able to arrest the growth of oppression and coerciveness which he has designed to provide himself with a sense of security—false and costly as it may be.

Ironically, man to be truly free must be able to say no to himself in the name of a higher yes. It is the task of traditional religion as well as other philosophies of life to show the way by which the sacred and eternal criteria of truth may shine through and become relevant to personal as well as social life.

> The acceptance of the sacred is an existential paradox: it is saying "yes" to a no; it is the antithesis of the will to power; it may contradict interests and stand in the way of satisfying inner drives.
>
> To our sense of power the world is at our disposal, to be exploited to our advantage. To accept the sacred is an acknowledgement that certain things are *not available to us, are not at our disposal.*[125]

An awareness as to what is sacred and eternal is necessary to shatter the flimsiness and false security of self-sufficiency and egoism. Such awareness is necessary in order to enable man to accept the doubt, risk, and insignificance of life that he otherwise attempts to conceal at the cost of degrading himself in his belief that he is either everything (sin) or nothing (neurosis*).

FAITH

Through the exercise of faith man finds perhaps one way amongst others by which he may transcend his condition of doubt, insignificance, and uncertainty. He may become confident about himself, paradoxically, when he no longer believes himself to be the source of his confidence. Hence, faith implies the overcoming of self-sufficiency and thereby doing away with the false security by which man attempts to avoid the facts of his all-pervasive sense of insignificance. Ironically, man may only truly become himself when he is able to appeal to a standard beyond himself that allows for the acceptance of his finite being. Faith allows man to transcend himself—to believe that he is needed rather than in his needs. Only in relating himself

---

* Both these positions become strategies which lead to the oppression of one's fellow man in the quest for consensus, acceptance, and conformity based on the illusion that thereupon doubt, risk, and uncertainty can be eliminated.

to ultimate meaning does he have the possibility of transcending himself.

If he is able to establish this faith he will have the possibility of transcending the anxiety and doubt that plague him when his convictions are based simply upon the dictum, "What is true is mine." Faith thus allows man the possibility to overcome the problem of self-centeredness and self-sufficiency as subtly manifested in the universal conditions of sin and neurosis. In turn, expediency and self-sufficiency may well be transcended when man is now able to recognize the flimsiness of his sense of sovereignty and presumptuousness.

Both sin and neurosis represent man's effort to lose himself in his self-centeredness and thereby avoid the element of risk, uncertainty, insignificance, and failure. These conditions inherent in life are brought to mind by the transiency of Time coupled with the impossible challenge of Evil that lies before each individual as well as each nation. It is therefore in the securing of faith in meaning beyond himself as well as his nation—a faith that transcends the conditions of man's finitude that allows him to accept the element of risk and insignificance in life. Risk and insignificance becomes acceptable only when one is convinced

> . . . that the death of the flesh annihilates the body which belongs to space and consciousness which belongs to time but it cannot annihilate that which constitutes the foundation of life; the special relation of every creature to the world.[126]

If man is to be free he must be willing to accept a morality of risk. Faith is based not on knowledge but on its abrogation.[127] After all, the father of faith went out without knowing where he was going. He did not have to know. A morality of risk is further inseparable from the creative nature of life. A morality of risk is based on the principle of love rather than in the quest for certainty as expressed in the self-love of sin and neurosis:

> Love is the answer to theproblem of moralisms and morality. Love transforms the moralism of authority into a morality of risk.[128]

It is in the principle of Love therefore by which man is able to unite the Truth of the Unconditional with the conditional of man's life situation. It is through the principle of Love that man is able to relate himself to the Eternal—and thereby transcend the doubt and uncertainty of life so that he may withstand the risks of freedom. Love moves him beyond self-love.

EPILOGUE

The ideas set forth in this book are already several years of age and with the passage of time and experience both their implication and meaning seem more lucid to myself; the intent of this epilogue is to afford a similar opportunity for the reader. In other terms I wish to harvest some of the fruits of what may at best have only been evident as burgeoning seeds when I initially undertook this work. However, if my assumptions in this regard are fallacious then let this epilogue serve only as a simple conclusion and summation of my ideas.

I have throughout this work insisted on purpose, strategy, and tactics as comprising the core element of human conduct. Uses, ends, and meanings rather than causes and mechanisms are basic to our comprehension of both individual and collective levels of conduct. More specifically, these tactics and strategies are simply the means by which oppression, intimidation, and coercion are both perpetuated and concealed. Nevertheless, that they characterize and typify personal, group, and national relationships in all its dimensions is an indisputable fact of life. Oppression, as I have hoped to make indisputably clear, reflects the insecurity of man's life rather than his evil instinctual nature.

In this vein the conduct of the patient who encounters the

psychiatrist in its core dimension reflects the outcome of one who has lived through the experience of oppression and intimidation. I do not regard him as sick in the traditional sense of the word; conversely, I consider his problems as essentially similar to those of any other individual or group whose ways of life are closely linked to their condition of oppression—whether he be Black, Jew, colonized, servant, worker, and so forth.

To pursue further the matter of the patient and the phenomen of oppression; it is my contention that no matter what the outward appearance of the symptom or syndrome it becomes the task of the psychiatrist to reveal as well as analyze the meaning of the tactics of manipulation and coercion that inevitably underline the symptom which in turn promotes and fosters the life style or plan of the individual. The patient may either be the oppressed or oppressor. I would suppose that as the disadvantages of oppression are less obvious and therefore appear to be more convenient (and at the outset, at least, less disconcerting) it would be logical to assume that the vast majority of patients who seek psychiatric assistance are those who bear the brunt of oppression. But let us not forget that ultimately neither the master nor the slave is free and that they will both inevitably be caught in the same ugly web.

What is most crucial in our attempt to comprehend these well-nigh universal strategies of manipulation and oppression is that man cannot live without self-esteem. In other terms, the manipulation of one man by the other—whether it be in the more conventional forms of master-slave relationships, worker-management arrangements, husband-wife associations, or those of a somewhat more idiosyncratic mode that we commonly define as a psychiatric problem—typify the human condition of our day. Manipulation and oppression—no matter the form—are man's time-worn strategies by which he hopes to use and exploit the "Other"—either through tactics of submission or domination—and thereby seek to gain his acceptance that he believes to be the only means by which he is able to maintain his self-esteem.

Now to return to our patient. He as any other individual or group who is oppressed often counts heavily on strategies and tactics of appeasement, self-humiliation and debasement (all of which are consistent with his symptoms, whether they be depressive, obsessive, or phobic, as well as his feelings) in order to ingratiate himself and thereby win the acceptance of the oppressor. In a word, the task of the psychiatrist is to render the individual before him exquisitely aware of the awesome risks and consequences of appeasement and capitulation. The implicit alternative of psychotherapy is to point to the possibility that the patient may opt to overtly challenge and confront his experience of oppression and therefore contend with the risks that he may find less perilous than those of capitulation. In other terms, the task of the psychiatrist can be no more than to render the patient aware of his strategies whereby he attempts to eschew the task of responsibility and choice; in essence it is this that is the core neurotic problem. Conversely and perhaps bluntly, it cannot matter to the psychiatrist qua psychiatrist (if he is to fulfill his main task of freeing the patient so that he openly assumes accountability for his actions) whether—as in the words of the prophet Elijah—the patient before him chooses God or Baal; that he count on himself rather than the "Other."

We now arrive at an impasse. Does it suffice for the oppressed in whatever category he may be to simply choose to save himself? Is it possible that through such means we may envision the resolution of the problem of oppression? I believe not, for in the words of Hillel, if man only saves himself, then who is he? Parenthetically, I may add at this point that the unavoidable limitations of the role of the therapist whose task at the very most can only be that of helping the client "save" himself becomes readily obvious.

Man may not permit himself to believe that he need simply be able to choose and decide and thereby automatically transcend the problem of oppression; for if his choice is one of evil rather than good he will inevitably trap himself in the quagmire of oppression and manipulation. How then do we distinguish between the commitment to good and to evil at least from the perspective of oppression? The latter may have the appearance of beginning by choice but ends by establishing both people and things (finite entities) as necessities in his effort to allay anxiety and maintain his self-esteem; yet such action inevitably compounds the cycle of oppression as the self becomes enslaved to one of these objects. The former means to opt for ultimate meaning where people or things remain as choices; if necessary we are prepared to do without them. This is possible as an alternative only to the extent that we possess the faith and *choose* to face the existential anxiety wherein we commit ourselves to Time (infinity) and link ourselves with the Eternal.

NOTES

[1] J. P. Sartre, *Being and Nothingness* (New York: Philosophical Library, 1956), p. 479.

[2] H. Bergson, *Two Sources of Morality and Religion* (New York: Doubleday, 1955), p. 204.

[3] Sartre, *op cit.*

[4] E. Becker, *Revolution in Psychiatry* (New York: Free Press, 1964).

[5] J. Ortega y Gasset, *Man and People* (New York: Norton, 1957).

[6] *Ibid.*

[7] D. Lee, *Freedom and Culture* (Englewood Cliffs, New Jersey: Prentice-Hall, 1959).

[8] H. Vaihinger, *The Philosophy of "As If"* (London: Routledge & Kegan Paul, 1942).

[9] R. Benedict, *Patterns of Culture* (New York: Houghton Mifflin, 1934).

[10] E. Becker, *Birth and Death of Meaning* (New York: Free Press of Glencoe, 1962).

[11] E. Cassirer, *An Essay on Man* (New Haven: Yale, 1944), p. 25.

[12] E. Sapir, *Culture, Language and Personality* (Berkeley: California, 1966).

[13] Frantz Fanon, *Black Skin, White Masks* (New York: Grove, 1967).

[14] Becker, *op cit.*, Chapter 6.

[15] T. Parsons, "Social Structure and the Development of The Personality," *Psychiatry*, 21 (1958) p. 321.

[16] Benedict, *op cit.*

[17] G. H. Mead, *The Social Psychology of George Herbert Mead* (Chicago: U. of Chicago, 1934).

[18] J. P. Sartre, Foreword to *The Traitor* by André Gorz (London: Calder, 1960), pp. 14–15.

[19] W. R. Fairbairn, *An Object-Relations Theory of the Personality* (New York: Basic Books, 1962), p. 31.

[20] E. Fromm, *Man for Himself: An Inquiry into the Psychology of Ethics* (New York: Holt, Rinehart & Winston, 1947).

[21] E. Fromm, "Individual and Social Origins of Neurosis," *Amer. Soc. Rev.*, IX (Aug, 1944), pp. 380–384.

[22] A. Adler, *Social Interest: A Challenge to Mankind* (New York: Capricorn, 1964), p. 131.

[23] E. Fromm, *Escape from Freedom* (New York: Holt, Rinehart & Winston, 1941), p. 291.

[24] A. I. Hallowell, "The Self and Its Behavioral Environment" in *Culture and Experience* (Philadelphia: U. of Pennsylvania Press, 1955).

[25] S. Kierkegaard, *Fear and Trembling: Sickness Unto Death* (New York: Doubleday Anchor, 1954), p. 191.

[26] C. W. Mills, *Sociological Imagination* (New York: Oxford 1959).

[27] T. Veblen, *Theory of the Leisure Class* (New York: Mentor, 1954).

[28] E. Goffman, *Presentation of Self in Every Day Life* (New York: Doubleday Anchor, 1959).

[29] E. Fromm, *Man for Himself* (New York: Holt, Rinehart & Winston, 1947).

[30] R. Peters, *Concept of Motivation* (London: Routledge & Kegan Paul, 1958).

[31] Fairbairn, *op cit.*

[32] P. Berger, *Invitation to Sociology: A Humanistic Perspective* (New York: Doubleday Anchor, 1963), p. 96.

[33] F. Kafta, *The Penal Colony* (New York: Schocken, 1948).

[34] E. Goffman, *Stigma: Notes on the Management of Spoiled Identity* (New York: Prentice-Hall, 1963).

[35] J. P. Sartre, *The Anti-Semite and the Jew* (New York: Grove, 1962), p. 26.

[36] R. D. Laing, *The Politics of Experience* (New York: Pantheon, 1967).

[37] Allen B. Wheelis, *The Desert* (New York: Basic Books, 1970).

[38] *Ibid.*

[39] J. Ortega y Gasset, *The Revolt of the Masses* (New York: Norton, 1932).

[40] F. Fanon, *op cit.*, p. 218.

[41] G. Ryle, *Concept of the Mind* (New York: Barnes & Noble, 1949).

[42] *Ibid.*, p. 32.

[43] *Ibid.*

[44] *Ibid.*

[45] A. Adler, *Understanding Human Nature* (New York: World, 1927), p. 265.

[46] J. P. Sartre, *The Emotions* (New York: Philosoph. Lib., 1948).

[47] F. Fanon, *Wretched of the Earth* (New York: Grove, 1966).

[48] E. H. Carr, *What is History?* (New York: Knopf, 1963).

[49] Sartre, *op cit.*, p. 40.

[50] Carr, *op cit.*

[51] Mills, *Sociological Imagination.*

[52] C. W. Mills, *Power, Politics and People* (New York: Ballantine, 1939).

[53] C. W. Mills, *Causes of World War Three* (New York: Ballantine, 1958), p. 94.

[54] Baker Brownell, *The Human Community: Its Philosophy and Practice for a Time of Crisis* (New York: Harper & Row, 1950).

[55] Mills, *Causes of World War Three*, p. 172.

[56] R. Nisbet, *Community and Power* (New York: Oxford, 1962).

[57] *Ibid.*

[58] Adler, *Social Interest*, p. 172.

[59] T. S. Szasz, *The Myth of Mental Illness* (New York: Harper & Row, 1961).

[60] Becker, *op cit.*

[61] Adler, *op cit.*

[62] Ortega y Gasset, *op cit.*

[63] M. Buber, *Paths in Utopia* (Boston: Beacon, 1958).

[64] A. Huxley, *Brave New World* (New York: Harper & Row, 1946), p. 13.

[65] M. Buber, *Between Man and Man* (New York: Macmillan, 1965), p. 159.

[66] L. Kovar, "Reconsideration of Paranoia," *Psychiatry*, 29:3 (Aug. 1966), pp. 289–305.

67 M. Boss, *Meaning and Content of Sexual Perversion* (New York: Grune & Stratton, 1949).

68 J. P. Sartre, *Saint Genet* (New York: Mentor, 1964).

69 Ortega y Gasset, *op cit.*

70 Kierkegaard, *op cit.*, p. 160.

71 E. Becker, *Mills' Social Psychology and the Great Convergence on the Problem of Alienation in the New Sociology* (New York: Oxford, 1964).

72 Quoted in G. Grob, *The State and the Mentally Ill* (Chapel Hill: North Carolina, 1966), p. 3.

73 Szasz, *op cit.;* Laing, *op cit.;* A. Wheelis, *op cit.*

74 Benedict, *op cit.*

75 Ryle, *op cit.*, p. 16.

76 *Ibid*, p. 58.

77 *Ibid*, p. 45.

78 T. Sarbin, "On the Futility of the Proposition that Some People Be Labeled 'Mentally Ill,'" *Journal of Consulting Psychology*, 4, No. 5, (Oct. 1967), pp. 447–453.

79 Vaihinger, *op. cit.*

80 T. Szasz, "Nature of Pain," *AMA Archives of Neur. and Psych.*, 74:174. (1955).

81 G. Engel, "Psychogenic Pain and the Pain Prone Patient," *Amer. J. of Medicine*, XXVI 6 (July, 1959), pp. 899–918.

82 Ryle, *op cit.*, p. 202.

83 *Ibid*, p. 215.

84 *Ibid*, p. 168.

85 Berger, *op cit.*, p. 96.

86 Ryle, *op cit.*, p. 258.

87 Sartre, *op cit.*

88 E. T. Carlson and Norman Dain, "The Psychotherapy that was Moral Treatment" (Dec. 1960).

89 L. Tolstoi, *The Works of Lyof N. Tolstoi*, Vol. 7 (New York: Crowell, 1969), p. 296.

90 Mills, *op cit.*

91 M. Foucault, *Madness and Civilization* (New York: Random House, 1965), p. 68.

92 *Ibid*, p. 70.

93 H. J. Home, "The Concept of Mind," *Int. J. Psycho. Anal.*, 47, 42, (1966), p. 47.

94 S. Freud, *Collected Papers* (New York: Basic Books, Vol. 3, 1959).

95 *Ibid.*, V. 4, p. 63.

96 A. Adler, *Individual Psychology* (Totowa, New Jersey: Little-field, Adams 1963), p. 237.

97 A. C. MacIntyre, *The Unconscious* (London: Routledge & Kegan Paul; New York: Humanities Press, 1958).

98 M. D. Altschule, *Roots of Modern Society* (New York: Grune & Stratton, 1965), p. 123.

99 Fanon, *op cit.*, p. 93.

100 P. Tillich, "What is Basic in Human Nature," *Amer. J. of Psycho. Anal.*, 22:115–21, (1962).

101 P. Tillich, *The Shaking of the Foundations* (New York: Scribner, 1948).

102 R. Niebuhr, *Nature and Destiny of Man* (New York: Scribner, 1964), V. 2, p. 218.

103 *Ibid.*, p. 168.

104 A. Heschel, *The Insecurity of Freedom: Essays on Human Existence* (New York: Noonday, 1959), p. 189.

105 *Ibid.*, p. 157.

106 P. Tillich, *The Religious Situation* (New York: Meridian, 1956), p. 51.

107 M. Buber, *Israel and the World* (New York: Schocken, 1948).

108 A. Heschel, *Who Is Man* (Stanford, Cal.: Stanford U. 1965).

109 Ortega y Gasset, *op cit.*, p. 97.

110 Buber, *op cit.*, p. 33.

111 Ortega y Gasset, *op cit.*, p. 77.

112 P. Tillich, *Courage to Be* (New Haven: Yale, 1952).

113 *Ibid.*, p. 66.

114 F. Lilge, *The Abuse of Learning* (New York: Macmillan, 1948).

115 L. Tolstoi, *The Death of Ivan Ilych* (New York: New American Library, 1960).

116 R. Leifer, "Psychotherapy, Scientific Method and Ethics," *Amer. J. of Psychotherapy*, 1966), Vol. XX, p. 300.

117 T. Szasz, *The Ethics of Psychoanalysis* (New York: Basic Books, 1965).

118 Adler, *op cit.*, p. 201.

119 Cassirer, *op cit.*, p. 62.

120 Fanon, *op cit.*, p. 111.

121 Mills, *op cit.*, p. 188.

122 M. Buber, *Pointing the Way* (New York: Harper Torchbook, 1963), p. 175.

123 Niebuhr, *op cit.*, V. 2, p. 26.

[124] Ortega y Gasset, *op cit.*, p. 157.

[125] Heschel, *op cit.*

[126] L. Tolstoi, *op cit.*, p. 394.

[127] L. Shestov, *Athens and Jerusalem* (Athens, Ohio: Ohio, 1968).

[128] P. Tillich, *Theology of Culture* (New York: Oxford, 1964), p. 143.

ABOUT THE AUTHOR

Roy D. Waldman is Director of the Mental Health Unit of the Rutgers University Health Service and Assistant Professor of Psychiatry at the Rutgers Medical School. He is a graduate of New York University, his medical degree is from the University of Geneva, and his residency in psychiatry was at the Upstate Medical Center in Syracuse, New York, from 1962 to 1965.

The text of this book was set in Caledonia Linotype and printed by letterpress on Warren's #66 Antique manufactured by S. D. Warren Company, Boston, Massachusetts. Composed, printed and bound by H. Wolff Book Manufacturing Company Inc., New York, N.Y.